CW00481742

INDIA: PAST GLIMPSES OF COUNTRY LIFE

by

Charles M. Copland

Published by
MELROSE BOOKS
An Imprint of Melrose Press Limited
St Thomas Place, Ely
Cambridgeshire
CB7 4GG, UK
www.melrosebooks.com

First Edition published by Lewis Recordings, 1988
This Edition published by Melrose Books, 2006

Cover designed by Catherine McIntyre

ISBN10 1 905226 56 X
ISBN13 978 1 905226 56 6

Printed and bound in Great Britain by:
CPI Bath, Lower Bristol Road,
Bath, BA2 3BL, UK

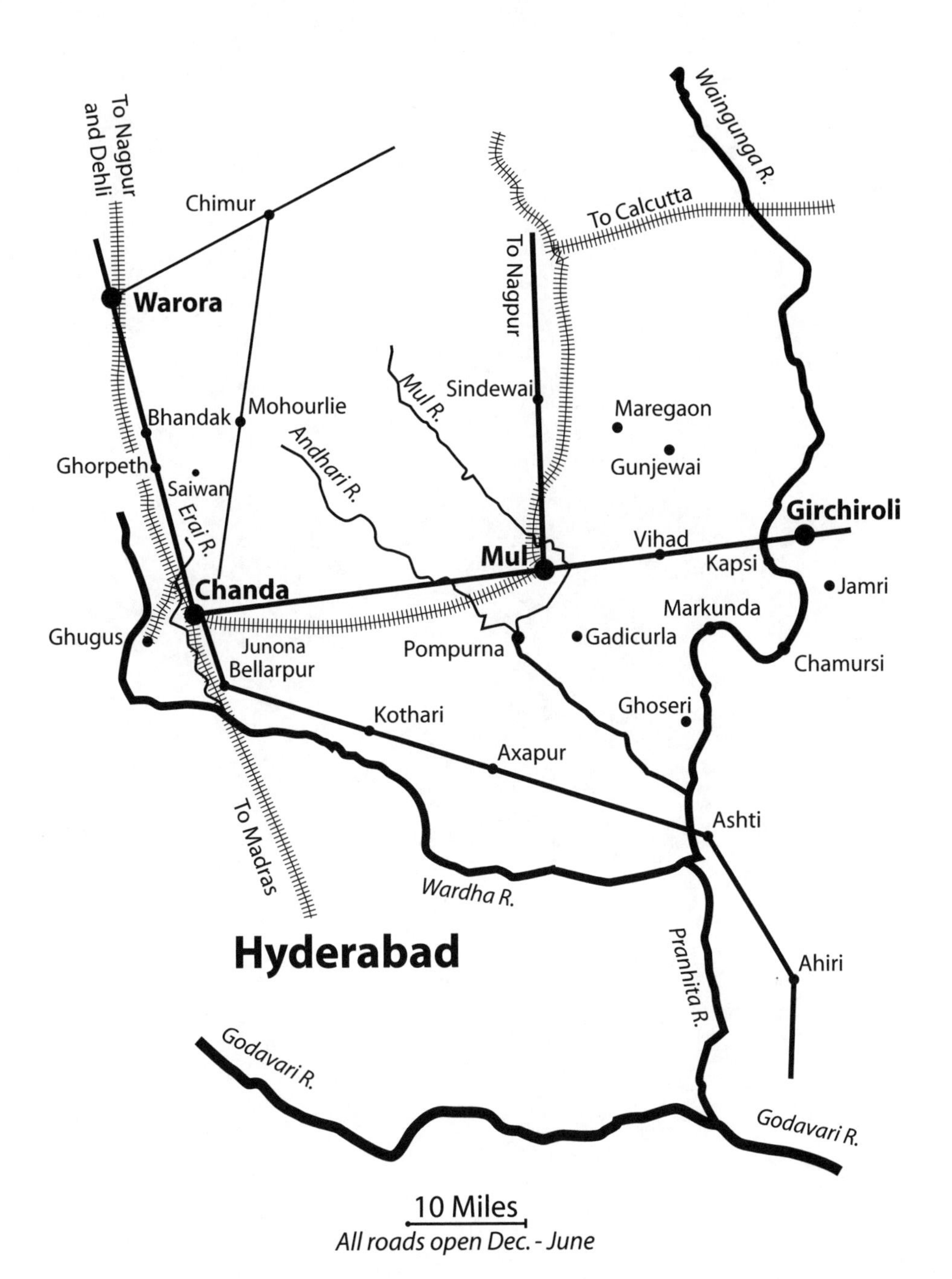

To Nagpur and Dehli
Chimur
Warora
Bhandak
Mohourlie
Ghorpeth
Saiwan
Erai R.
Chanda
Ghugus
Junona
Bellarpur
Andhari R.
Mul R.
Sindewai
To Nagpur
To Calcutta
Wainganga R.
Maregaon
Gunjewai
Girchiroli
Vihad
Mul
Kapsi
Jamri
Markunda
Gadicurla
Pompurna
Chamursi
Ghoseri
Kothari
Axapur
Ashti
To Madras
Wardha R.
Hyderabad
Pranhita R.
Ahiri
Godavari R.
Godavari R.
10 Miles
All roads open Dec. - June

PREFACE
by BISHOP LUSCOMBE

I am delighted to have been asked to write this Preface.

Twenty years ago, when I was Primus of the Scottish Episcopal Church, I was concerned that the record should not be lost of our church's Mission to Chanda over a period of nearly a century. It was then that I asked Canon Charles Copland to write an account of his time in India. He had been head of the Chanda Mission from 1942 until 1953 after serving on the staff there as a Mission priest.

The present book brings that account up to date and it is good that it should now be in more permanent form. Canon Copland was born in 1910 and the fact that he writes with such clarify is a matter for real congratulation.

He opens a window onto the life of a Scottish priest serving in India in the last century as well as giving a glimpse, as the title implies, into the closing years of the British Raj. To those of us who lived in the sub-continent at the time it will bring back vivid memories.

India, Past Glimpses of Country Life is the kind of book that is best treated as an anthology and read as a chapter at a time so as to get a lively sense of what was a hard, and yet immensely rewarding, life.

Edward Luscombe
✠ Kirkton of Tealing
October 2006

Revd. Nehemiah Goreh, 1872

Revd. Israel Jacob 1877

CONTENTS

THE CHANDA MISSION OF THE SCOTTISH EPISCOPAL CHURCH

The Primus asked me to bring the history of Chanda up-to-date. And with the history, I hope to give glimpses of the work from time to time.

It is not an easy task. I have clear memories of what happened between 1938 and 1953. Beyond that, on either side, I have largely to rely on the help of others. From very early days, the Head of the Mission used to send a full annual report back to the Mission Board in Edinburgh. It is a pity that most of these products of hard labour seem to have been thrown out – possibly at the time of removal from Drumsheugh Gardens to Grosvenor Crescent, or at the time of tidying up, or perhaps when it became the aim of the Board to take the whole world for its parish. At any rate, that full and official source of detail is not available. When I draw on my own experience, readers will appreciate that the experience of others has been very similar.

Dates are a difficulty. In the earlier records, there is sometimes uncertainty. At one time during the '39-'45 war, letters would take three months to arrive, so that what is reported in print in Scotland in one year, may well have happened in the previous year.

The Scottish Guardian, for long the weekly paper of our Scottish Church, was very friendly to Chanda, and much information has been gleaned from its pages. The publishers, Messrs David Winter of Dundee, have most generously welcomed quotation. There is also a good deal to be found in **The Scottish Churchman,** once our monthly magazine, in the **Scottish Chronicle,** and in the pages of the old **Foreign Mission Chronicle**. I shall also refer to books by Bishop Chatterton, by Bishop Wood, and by the Revd Dr K W Mackenzie, DSO. The CWMA that was, Links as it now is, has always been a true handmaid to the Mission, and their archives have proved a mine of information, and their help most valuable.

Chanda, or Chandrapur as it is now called, was a government district in the very middle of India, about half the size of Scotland. Put a finger on the middle of a map of India and you have Chanda, with Nagpur to the north and Hyderabad to the south. In 1870 the

Mission was started by the efforts of the Revd G T Carruthers, son of an editor of the **Inverness Courier,** and Chaplain of Nagpur. At that time, Chanda was in the Diocese of Calcutta, as was the whole continent of Australia. Mr Carruthers' first agent in Chanda was a Mr Hereford, a retired officer of the Public Works Department (PWD) who built a little school in 1870. Almost at once an Indian took over. This was Fr Nehemiah Goreh in 1872, a Brahmin convert trained by the Cowley Fathers in Poona.

"They tell of him as a slim figure in a white cassock. Round his neck was a rosary of wooden beads and attached to it a wooden cross. In his hand he held a heavy wooden cross higher than his head, and on this he leaned. People passed and re-passed, going about their business, but he stood still, taking no notice. But as he stood silent there, for an hour perhaps or more, the people noted, watched, stood around, waiting shyly. For whether he were a Christian or not, at least he was a Brahmin. Then at last, when a circle had gathered round him in the cool of the evening, he preached to them of Christ."

Fr Goreh made a considerable impression on the people, but had few baptisms. The descendants of his first convert, the Moon family, are still in Chandrapur. They have been valuable members of the Christian Community.

It was in 1871 that the Metropolitan Bishop specifically asked the Episcopal Church of Scotland to take on the work. Fr Goreh left in 1874 but revisited Chanda several times. In Scotland he once stayed with the Revd J Comper in Aberdeen. Fr Goreh was succeeded by Israel Jacob, then a catechist, who trained for the ministry at Indore, made deacon in 1877, and was ordained priest in 1882. He was very much on his own, and had little guidance. Yet Mr Jacob won the confidence of the whole community. The DC – the District Commissioner, the senior government officer – appointed him an honorary magistrate. Canon Lawson wrote of him: "Mr Jacob's task was one of peculiar difficulty, as he was practically single-handed and unsupported by any resident European in the midst of that great heathen community. If the Mission languished during this period, he at least upheld a high standard of personal Christian character and enjoyed the respect of the people to a remarkable degree."

In 1898 the Revd Alex Wood, an Aberdeenshire man and curate at Forfar, responded to Bishop Wilkinson's call and offered to serve in Chanda. Like Ninian going to Tours, Wood went first to the Dublin University Mission in Ranchi before moving on to Chanda. There he found there was almost no mission at all: "Only the history of a Mission that had failed for eight and twenty years." There wrote the young man.

Alex Wood was fortunate in finding nowhere to stay except a small house within the city walls. There he was seen by the people, mixed with the people, got to know the people. From that developed his running fight for the lower castes, winning for them in the end places in the government high school. Wood was fortunate too in the onset, in 1899, of the great famine. That, too, threw him among the people. He was asked to supervise the government road works south of Chanda. He took over the care of famine orphans variously reported as being 250 or 300. All this earned him within a year or two of his arrival, the Gold Kaiser-i-Hind Medal.

The arrival of Wood and the famine marked a new beginning for the Mission. Of the children who survived, several became outstanding leaders of the Christian community in later years. Among them may be mentioned Monica bai Luther, matron of the girls' hostel and mother of a bishop of Bombay; Shimon Damle honoured and respected head of our boys' primary school in Chanda and father of a head of the government high school; Reuben Chandeker clerk and clerk of the works and reliable pillar of strength to many heads of the Mission, and the Revd Habel Jagtap, revered parish priest and father-in-law of a Bishop of Nagpur.

Chanda's need drew help. The Revd G D Philip joined Wood in 1901, and he was soon followed by Mrs Aitken from Aberfoyle and Miss Smyth. It may be of interest to know which charges sent help to Chanda. The Revd G D Philip, later a much honoured Canon of Nagpur, had served in Auchterarder, at St John's in Perth, and at St Andrew's in St Andrews. Miss Smyth, from the UMCA, later became Mrs. Philip.

This was a time of building – for the girls' hostel and a bungalow for the ladies; the Montgomery bungalow and the Claud Hamilton Orphanage. The names suggest strong Ayrshire support. Both these buildings still stand and still give good service in busy use. St Andrew's Church, within the city of Chanda, later enlarged, was consecrated in 1903 on St Andrew's Day. About this time was started the custom of the hostel boys coming down to church every morning, and the girls from a little further outside the city walls. At first it was every day, and then on Tuesdays and Fridays as well as on Sundays.

Chandu, the leader of the Kabir Panthis, became an enquirer about 1903.

In his book "Forest Life in India", J W Best, later Conservator of Forests, gives a glimpse of life in Chanda about this time: "Chanda Station itself was different from others that I was appointed to later in my service. Perhaps it was the influence of the good Padres of the Scottish Episcopal Mission which had a strong and healthy Mission there. It may have been the very remoteness of the place that made European Officers realize that they were strangers in a strange land and must pull together, for Chanda was essentially a happy family station. One heard of no rows then in spite of the appalling heat. This I did not appreciate till later, but when I visited it again after many years when roads and railways made up to and beyond Chanda – it boasted of two railway stations – there was still a Scotch Padre (J R McKenzie) whose influence, social and religious, tended to the smooth running of the place. Chanda owes much to those same Padres, Philip, Wood and the two Mackenzies. It is presumption on my part to praise them."

Now Wood was able to give more time to getting out and about on evangelistic touring. He stationed the Revd W Patwardhan, a Brahmin convert, in the south at Ahiri, the main centre of the Gond Country. In time he became persona grata throughout the remains of the southern Gond kingdom. Mr Patwardhan produced a Gondi grammar, complimentary to that made by Mrs C M Copland's grandfather, the Revd H D Williamson, for the northern kingdom in Mandla. Sadly, Mr Patwardhan never managed to lead the Gonds to Christ. That may have been due to the influence of the Gond Rajah, or it may have been because Canon Patwardhan never received the hoped for support of a European missionary to live among the Gonds.

Warora, then at the end of the railway, forty-two miles north of Chanda, was an obvious choice for an outstation. When the government mines there were closed, the big solid institute building was handed over to the Mission. It was never quite clear how fully it was handed over, but the Mission grew food there during the '39-'45 war, it is still in possession of the Church, and is more fully used than ever. The Revd Joseph Randhevi, BA, took charge of what is now St Mary's Church.

The railway moved forward to Bhandak, sixteen miles from Chanda. So in 1902, a small school was built here, for many years now continuing in use as a church. This is the site of the ancient city of Bhadrawati, and the extensive remains can still be seen. I only saw the ruins on one occasion, when Mr H Medd the architect of New Delhi Cathedral very kindly came to advise us on how to extend St Andrew's Church. That was shortly before the outbreak of the '39-'45 war. Cuthbert Hall had invited us to go snipe shooting around the old buildings. That was probably the last time we shot snipe: thereafter

Bhandak Church

we had to produce bigger results for scarce cartridges! Bhandak or Bhadrawati became the site of a large munitions factory.

The railway came to Chanda and then moved forward along the line of the road Alex Wood helped to build, to Bellarpur or Bellarshah ten miles to the south. Later it went on to Madras. Again at Bellarshah there are mines. The only fireplace we knew of in Chandrapur was in the DC's bungalow. But at the collieries people cooked on coal fires, and the smell of them always seemed strange. Bellarpur got a school and a catechist. For many years Thomas Ghadge was headmaster, and his family became known in Chanda and in Nagpur. St Luke's Church in Bellarshah was in the charge of the Revd Luke Singam from Ghugus.

1922: Ghugus was another colliery village, west of the road between Chandrapur and Bhandak. Around 1911 it got its railway, but never in our time a road. Visitors were pushed along the line on a trolley, to the mine headquarters where we were allowed to put up. The Eucharist was celebrated in the school, before it was handed over, and then in the post office which was the headmaster-catechist's house. To him, Prabhaker Sathe, must go most human credit for the steady and exceptional growth of this little Christian community. Many of the miners were Telegu, and always among them were some Christians. To their help and support credit too must be given. They have built their own church, St Thomas'. The congregation was later in the charge of the Revd V B Waidande. At one time we heard of forty baptisms at Ghugus.

After independence in 1947, Prabhaker – who was later ordained – appealed to us to take a specially deserving Hindu boy into the hostel, so that he could go to high school. That was an unheard of thing to do. As well as being good for the boy, we thought it might be good for the world to see how broadminded we were. The boy was admitted. Whether the world noticed or not, I don't know, but as Prabhaker may have hoped, when he had finished high school, the boy asked to be baptised. Madyania became one of the leaders of the Christian community.

Ghugus trolley

I specially remember two other boys from Ghugus. Their mother was a widow, and they lived in the village separate from the colliery quarters, and no doubt they were poorer than any of the colliery workers. The roof of their house was so low that I had to remain kneeling throughout the Eucharist, using their grindstone as an altar. They were outstanding athletes, and they made good in the world. More importantly, they became leaders in the worshipping Christian community. David John got a job in the railway at Bombay. He played cricket for the railway, which was quite something in Bombay. He became a member of the Executive Committee of the Church of India and after reunion in 1970 continued on the Executive Committee of the United Church. He became a qualified solicitor. My wife and I had the privilege of staying the night with him in Bombay when we returned to Chandrapur in 1970 for the centenary celebrations.

The Revd J R McKenzie from Coates Hall (later of St Margaret's, Easter Road, Greenock, and Crieff) joined the Mission in 1909 and quickly made a name for himself. He carried on through the '14-'18 war, and returned to be head when Canon Wood was nominated as Bishop of Chota Nagpur in 1920. He retired again in 1931. The Revd Dr K W Mackenzie, after distinguished war service in the RAMC and missionary service on the North West Frontier, did a tour of service in Chanda 1921–3. In 1923 the Revd J D Bisset came out after ministering at Stirling and Milngavie (later of Monifieth, Drumtochty and Doune). Mr Bisset worked in Chanda and in Nagpur, and then as a Diocesan Chaplain. To the very end of his life he had a great love for Chanda.

Also in 1923 the Revd A Clark Barnacle joined the Mission from Edinburgh Cathedral. Presumably the heat proved too much and he could not stay.

Catechumens from Vichoda, 1936

It was around 1925 that the last of the strategic outstations was developed, with a small and very hot bungalow at Mul, almost due east of Chanda on the main Nagpur road, some thirty miles from Chandrapur. Thus Mul is a useful staging post for work on the east side of the district, looking north to the boundary, east over the Waingunga, and south to the Gond country. It is on the narrow gauge railway from Calcutta. The Towers family nobly lived in this bungalow for a time, and later the Revd Samuel Sukare was stationed there with oversight of the Christian community at Gadicurla.

In 1927 the Revd E R Griffiths Jones from Falkirk and Old St Paul's in Edinburgh came to the Mission, stayed as Head when Canon J R McKenzie retired in 1931, and left in 1934. Then the Rector of Dumfries, Dr K W Mackenzie, came once more to the rescue. The Revd A Armstrong from Christ Church, Glasgow, served in the Mission 1931–6.

At Epiphany in 1936 there was an influx of some hundred catechumens from Vichoda and around, seven miles from Chanda. It was a great happiness to all that this took place when Alex Wood, now Bishop of Nagpur, was confirming some forty candidates in his old Mission.

Later in 1936 the Revd H F A Treble joined the Mission from Clydebank, and succeeded Dr Mackenzie as Head in 1939.

Jogi Sant of Sakherwai was a religious leader among the Mahars, but of lesser calibre than Chandu. A small church was built there, just beyond the tank outside the village. I recollect a difficulty of distant direction: the Convener of the Board in Scotland wanted the Church made with mud bricks, but without the lime plaster we would have put on as a protection from driving rain. Sad to say, in time the lower bricks decayed and the walls went down. There were only three or four families at first, delightful people, weaving, and cultivating their fields. On one occasion, Hurri was told off for missing a Eucharist.

"But Sahib, I had to go and sell my cloth. I went to the bazaar at Bhandak, and I joined in the Eucharist there. Was that alright?"

Later, poor Hurri got it again; he would have to leave for another bazaar before the service.

"O.K. Come before you go, I'll be here. Come at 4, 5, or 6 – whenever you like."

I was camping in the priest's room at the church, or more accurately sleeping just outside the west door. Hurri and his bullock cart came about 4 a.m. I put my head in a bucket, and soon afterwards the Eucharist began. Hurri got to the bazaar on time.

Gadicurla was seven miles off any road, somewhere south of Mul. Cuthbert Hall and I arrived in Chanda in the autumn of 1938. (Hall

'The Promised Land'

from St Margaret's Newlands, later Kirkcudbright; Copland from Forfar and Ardrossan, later Arbroath and Oban). We had seven years of almost incessant evangelistic touring without any obvious results. It was in Mul district that Stephen Master made his last tour. He was a senior catechist, and had served in the '14-'18 war. He got fever, and we tried to send him home, but he insisted on continuing and preaching. Not so long afterwards he died. I think it was Wamanrao Ramteke, later ordained, who first explored this part of the district. I remember with him looking out from the local hill over "the promised land". Wherever we went, we were helped by these efficient and devoted catechists. Later, when contact had been made, the biblewomen and the ladies followed. It was only after all those years that we saw our first catechumens, two or three brave families from the Mahars of Gadicurla. And they turned shy. On the first date fixed, someone had fever and could not come. The next time a mother-in-law was ill. Finally they plucked up their joint courage and became catechumens. It was easy to tend them and teach them, until the rains approached. What should we do? Bajerao Madame, the catechist who had had a chief share in their teaching, said he would camp alone in the village in a tent through the rains. (In a dry bungalow, things went mouldy in the rains, what would it be like in a tent?) It was a thing unheard of. Most people would have said it was impossible. Bajerao did it. Naturally the caste people would not allow him to use their well. He had to use the tank water, used for every sort of washing – human and animal. He survived. And the catechumens grew happily to baptism. We built a little house, with a chapel on the veranda. I think Bishop Hannay consecrated the altar. Bajerao and his family went and lived there. Later, Bajerao had the joy of being ordained.

Saiwan, east of the Chanda-Bhandak road, was probably the next village to produce catechumens, and to get a little house for a catechist and for worship. Joseph Master took up residence, with his wife, Rujilla bai, carrying on the work begun by Cuthbert Hall and George Wells and their helpers. George Wells made an improvement on the Gadicurla plan, by putting in an east window, an open cross one brick wide. There was a smaller group of catechumens at Ghorpeth, only three miles away on the main road to Bhandak. They could easily join Saiwan for Sunday worship. Today, the village of Saiwan has ceased to exist, being done away for some government project.

In India not many people had clocks, and there was a good deal of give and take in time about arriving for a service. We were generously given some railway line from time to time, to act as church bells. Only those who have worked with railway lines will realise the weights we had to deal with. I remember once setting out on cycle to take eighteen inches of line to Sakherwai. All this area is black cotton soil, and in many places one could see the sad effects of erosion – gullies opening up where they had never been before. Of late there must have been a shower. When I left the road to do the last few miles through the fields, I was quickly bogged down. Taking off the mudguards only got me another few hundred yards. I was tempted to leave the cycle standing up in the mud. Had I done so, probably I and the line would have sunk. In time, and in mud, the bit of line and I did reach the church. Railway bells are not musical, but they are demanding in their call. Chanda had two feet, Durgapur had a yard. Ajmir, nine hundred miles to the north but still in the Nagpur Diocese, and the Revd P Ashwin, later of the SPG, offered to send us a real church bell. The bell may have started, but it never arrived.

During the '39-'45 war the government gave us six and a half acres of agricultural land at Vihad, on the road east from Mul towards the Waingunga, on condition that we opened a school. There I made an architectural mistake; I wanted a long unimpeded veranda, with a

Sakerwai

Holy Cross, Gudicurla, the first of the house churches.

The Coplands, Bajerao Madame and his family,
Jogi of Sakherwai (centre), Hurri and Paulus Krishna.

teak trunk about twenty feet long to hold up the roof. The tekedar and Ruben Master thought the span too long, and of course in time it sagged. We had to put up a teak pole to hold it up in the middle. But the great cross on the gable was there for all to see.

About the same time the Mission bought a small plot and built a school at Kapsi, about five miles off the Vihad road, but conveniently on the small irrigation system.

In 1949, we bought a foothold at Dhanora, across the Waingunga and only ten miles short of the eastern district boundary. This might provide an opening to the Gond country from the north.

Vihad school.

CHANDU

Alex Wood must have been thrilled when Chandu, the Guru of the Kabir Panthis in Chanda, asked to learn about the Christian religion, then for instruction, and then for baptism. That was some time around 1903-1904. Chandu was in fact the leader of the Kabir Panthis throughout the whole province and perhaps beyond. The Kabir's teaching was an amalgam of Hinduism and Muslim teaching, but they worshipped one God.

When Chandu was to be baptised, it is said that his followers wanted some visible assurance that he renounced the old ways and entered the new. Possibly the Christians wanted that assurance too. So, one night, just before midnight, Christians and Kabir Panthis assembled near the ancient city wall. A fire was kindled, and at a given signal Chandu advanced and flung into the flames books representing the Hindu, the Muslim, and the Kabir teaching. He and his followers turned to Christ.

Chandu with Dr. Mackenzie and H F A Treble

It was not until 1911 that a government grant of land was secured for the new community, at Durgapur some three or four miles north of Chanda. In 1923, after Dr Mackenzie had been living in the village for some time, the growing community decided to build a church, and later, it was Dr Mackenzie who planned a beautiful extension. He also inspired the building of a tank for water for the cattle and the fields.

Chandu was a great and an attractive personality. Wherever he went he had a big walking stick or an umbrella, and always he was followed by his disciple Ardku. He was charming with the missionaries, and no doubt accepted their guidance. Then with a chuckle, I am sure, he went his own way with regard to his continued (and still unbaptised) following throughout the province.

With people and families moving about less than in Britain, I suppose it was easier in Chanda to notice how Christians, great in some way, passed on their attributes to their children. One could see that in many families. Chandu was succeeded as Patel (government headman) by his son Tarachand – a man charming, delightful, staunch and influential. Tarachand's son carried on the tradition, is known in Scotland and became a distinguished priest in Nagpur Diocese – the Revd Murlider Dhoteker. Chandu's daughter, Ruth Kamla bai, also has her father's friendliness and charm. She married one of our headmasters, Prabhudas Chandekar. Their son, Remesh, is ordained, has a Ph.D, and teaches in the Christian College at Indore. So one could go on.

It is I think worth reproducing what Dr Mackenzie wrote in the **Scottish Guardian** of 23rd June, 1944:

Building Sakerwai Church

"There passed away on May 14th at his own village of Durgapur one of the most interesting personalities of our Chanda mission.

"Chandu was the "Guru" (religious adviser) of a little poverty-stricken group, living outside one of the gates of Chanda City, when Bishop Wood first made contact with them. They were Kabir Panthis, that is, followers of Kabir, a Panjabi sage of the early 16th Century. Some excised jungle land was eventually obtained for them three miles out of Chanda, and there they started a little Christian Community of five families. This has become the flourishing village of Durgapur with some six hundred souls, of which Chandu was the Headman, officially known as Patel.

"Chandu was a most engaging individual, with a ready laugh, always at his best when his village was being visited by the Bishop or other notable visitor, when he presided at the reception and inevitable garlanding with an eloquent and dignified speech of welcome.

"Much more important was Chandu's religious influence, not only in his own village, but widespread throughout the district. He never lost the influence the tenets of Kabir made upon him, and to the last made frequent tours among the Kabirpanthis to be found in the province. Many were inclined to look askance at these visitations, for Chandu never learned to read the scriptures with any facility, though he was a devout communicant and worshipper, yet amid the extraordinary complexity of India's religious background, one felt that even a partially informed zeal was not to be despised, and zeal there certainly was.

"One of the most interesting things about this man, a very practical cultivator and man of business, was the influence of a sage who lived some 450 years before. Kabir desired to combine the Hindu and the Mahommedan religions, and his chief disciple was Nanak Singh, the founder of the Sikh religion, which at the outset did fuse some elements of Moslems and Hindus in the Punjab. Moved by a similar desire, Chandu at one time organised great conventions at his village of all the Indian religions, where all and sundry came and lived, and debated in a vast hall of bamboo matting for days at a time. On the first occasion we had received no previous warning, but took the precaution of sending strong parties of Christian speakers to seize the opportunity of presenting the Christian faith to a wide audience. When, however, this tended to become an annual fixture, the Mission had to place a ban upon the meetings, and Chandu, who had been billed as Chairman at a big meeting of this kind in Chanda City, had the courage, out of loyalty to the Mission, to break off in the middle and return to his village. Without his presence the meeting came to an abrupt end.

"Many will miss his cheerful personality, and his village a wise controller."

With regard to that meeting which ended abruptly, I sense the influence of that stalwart doyen of Chanda's clergymen, the Revd Haberjee Bhalerao.

When Chandu died, his parish priest, the Revd Canon Patwardhan, a Brahmin convert, reported that there was a proposal to bury the leader in a sitting position, and that that was wrong.

St Michael's, Durgapur

So the position was explained to the people, and I think all was well. The following Sunday I was specially invited to celebrate the Eucharist in Durgapur. We gave thanks for Chandu's life and leadership, and I bade the people pray that the Lord would have mercy on him and on all the faithful departed.

From early days, Durgapur had a mission school. But in the 40s and 50s the village did not even have a post office. Now it is a big town and has its own high school and a large open-cast coal mine. Recently it was reported that Durgapur had the highest literacy rating in the whole of the state of Maharashtra – 96%.

ST. THOMAS', NAGPUR

St Thomas' congregation in Nagpur was undoubtedly a part of the Chanda Mission, and yet it was a good deal older than the Mission. This congregation, as a Tamil congregation mainly of the soldiers of the Madras Regiment stationed at Kamptee, was in existence in 1840. It was fortunate in having the help of good chaplains of Nagpur. St Thomas' has always been a leader, sometimes difficult to lead, and its members are leaders in the diocese today.

At least two of the congregation, Mr Sumant Ghadge and Mr Leonard Sukare, have represented the Diocese on the Synod of the Church of North India. It is typical of the relationship between St Thomas' and St Andrew's in Chandrapur that the same names occur in both the publications I have relied on. St Thomas' notes Mr K S Damle as head of a big government high school (not surprisingly it was in Chanda); Mr C A. Randhivi was head of the Financial Department of Madya Pradesh; Mr M M Shinde, a leader in the Home Guard. Chandrapur might have claimed them all! Bishop Luther was once headmaster of Bishop Cotton School in Nagpur, as was Mr T S Ghadge; Mr M M Jacob was headmaster of the Gardiner High School, a Scottish Presbyterian establishment in Nagpur.

Here I can only refer briefly to previous publications, and specially I commend to readers the Souvenir of Centenary Celebrations of the Chanda Mission, 1970, and the Golden Jubilee Souvenir of St Thomas', 1978.

In 1872 the Revd N D Prakasham was in charge. In 1877 the Revd S B Ashirvadam took over. Already there was vigorous evangelism, and schools followed. In 1909 Canon Philip came to Nagpur. He and Mrs Philip encouraged the existing work, started up All Saints Hostel for girls, and worked and planned for the building of a worthy church. The Revd B Silas was in charge of the Tamil congregation, and the Revd S Jadhav of the Maharashtrians. Both these names are well-known and respected in Chandrapur today.

Canon Philip saw the foundation of the new church laid in 1918, but he died – beloved by all – in 1925 shortly before the consecration of the new church on St Thomas' Day in that year.

St Thomas' was the first part of the Chanda Mission to "grow up" and be handed over to the Diocese. Scotland gave a small endowment. That was in 1946. Since then the congregation has gone from strength to strength.

Among its rectors, St Thomas' has numbered a bishop of Bombay and Naisk, a Bishop of Nagpur, and Canon Wasant Mategaonker, the first Indian Canon of Nagpur Diocese. The Canon was later Principal of Nasik Divinity School, and before his retirement a vicar near Birmingham.

SUPPORT FOR CHANDA

It has already been noted that Chanda was the first overseas missionary project undertaken by the Scottish Episcopal Church. First we became responsible for the Central Indian Mission; then that was pared down to sole responsibility for the evangelisation of Chanda District in the then Central Provinces. That must have meant responsibility for the evangelisation of one million people in a district with ancient religious and cultural traditions. The district was about half the size of Scotland.

Very soon, however, the Episcopal Church made an additional promise, this time to help with the missionary work in Kaffraria (St John's Diocese) in South Africa. There lay the seeds of possible rivalry. Every penny of financial help for Chanda had to come from Scotland. Kaffraria had several English diocesan Kaffraria Missionary Associations to aid them, and some of these dioceses probably had more communicants than the whole of our Church. Kaffraria also had some Sisters, and the Cowley Fathers, working in their midst. In the early days, before Kaffraria or St. John's Diocese became the first "Black Homeland", there were some seventeen thousand Europeans living in the Diocese. The backing for Kaffraria was massive. Yet it was perhaps unavoidable in Scotland that jealous eyes were sometimes cast on Chanda if they received from Scotland more money than did Kaffraria. And it was not always generally remembered that Chanda received help from nowhere else.

The financial tug-of-war in Scotland came to a head from time to time. April 3rd, 1925: **The Scottish Chronicle** reported: "A resolution of the Kaffraria committee, that the Block Grant to Kaffraria be raised to £2,500, and the additional information that if not conceded there might be serious consequences." For the sake of peace in our Scottish Church the Chanda committee was ready to reduce their grant by almost a fifth, but it would mean a European priest and a nurse could not be replaced, one Indian priest to go, Ahiri to be abandoned, and the Hospital work to be curtailed. In the end, the Chanda grant was kept at £5,000, but staff was to be reduced and "it should be clearly realized" that there can be no development of the work "unless additional income can be obtained from some other sources." Clearly the Editor of **The Scottish Chronicle** backed Kaffraria, while the convenor of the Board stressed Chanda's priority. The grant was held at £5,000 only after forceful speeches by Dr O' Flaherty, that doughty warrior the Revd W Collins (Lenzie), and by the Revd Dr K W Mackenzie.

The visit of the Primus (Bishop Robberds) soon followed. Although he was also keen on Kaffraria, he came back convinced of the primacy of Scotland's obligation to Chanda.

Trouble seems to have boiled up again in Scotland in 1934. A leading article in **The Scottish Guardian** underlined the difference in the obligations we had to Chanda and to Kaffraria: "To compare mission work in Chanda and in Kaffraria is futile; there is nothing to compare; there is only contrast. Our workers, European and native alike in Chanda need all the sympathy that we can offer them... our best of prayer and almsgiving." Shortly afterwards Bishop Derbyshire visited Chanda. And he got recruits on his return.

In 1946 Bishop Hannay planned a visit to Kaffraria, but before he sailed he was asked to extend his visit to Chanda as well.

In time, I believe Kaffraria and Chanda came to receive the same amount of block grant from Scotland, until our Overseas Mission Board got the idea that the whole world was our parish. Thereafter, we gave help here, there, and elsewhere as need was seen; often for five years, and then "Goodbye". That was clearly useful for many projects, but it did not greatly help continuous work. In Scotland it obviously broadened our horizons, but it may not have produced such determined interest and prayer as formerly.

No doubt there was some Kaffraria-Chanda difficulty in finding European staff. Kaffraria certainly recruited people from Scotland, but she could also draw on the English dioceses, on the Sisters, and on Cowley. Chanda had to rely on us in Scotland. Those who rightly criticised the lack of a grand sweep of evangelism over the whole district were not always in the forefront in encouraging offers of service, or in finding the cash to pay for it. Readers of this booklet may well judge that Chanda has indeed suffered from the lack of Europeans, in the days when they were needed to lead the evangelistic drive.

A European missionary's pay has never been very big – and a good thing, too. But members of the OM Board in Edinburgh may not have had much experience to draw on. There is a sad little letter from the 1920s, explaining that a married missionary could not live on the pay of a single man. That was put right. And in time the OM Board came to keep an eye on SPG pay, only they tended to get the news two or three years later. Then the OM Board came to rely – to our great benefit – on the SPG vetting women volunteers. The Selly Oak College also proved most helpful. The Chanda missionaries had one great advantage: they were exceptionally well taught in the missionary language school at Mahableshwar, and became fluent in Marathi. Many Kaffraria missionaries relied on interpreters.

Scotland's differing degrees of mission responsibility gave rise to minor difficulties. With so many English speakers at work, Kaffraria could often be writing to Scotland to tell how things were going, and to plead for some special project. With so few in Chanda, they mostly had other things to do. That may seem a small point, but it did carry weight in Scotland's parishes and therefore in Chanda. It certainly increased the typing speed of missionaries! With so many Europeans working in Kaffraria, in any year some could always be found on leave, to come and tell Scotland of the work. Whereas Chanda's few Europeans only came singly to Scotland once in five or even seven years. Both Missions were good at publicity, but Kaffraria obviously had the advantage. If a new school or a new hospital was opened anywhere in the diocese, that was reported in Scotland, and little Johnnie felt that his Lent savings had been well used. No one told him that he had only provided about one hundredth part of the school! Chanda would have bankrupted the Episcopal Church, if she had tried to keep pace.

The women's work parties were a great source of help – some working for Kaffraria, some for Chanda, and some very properly for both missions. They stitched and they sewed, and sent out great bales of shirts and jumpers and pullovers. And every stitch showed missionary zeal and interest. In Chanda, the arrival of the annual bale was a day of great rejoicing, promising warmth in winter. All that was fine, until the day when the government clapped on a huge tariff. Then it actually became cheaper to buy the clothes in India, rather than to pay the customs charges. Chanda had to say "Stop!" It could hardly be avoided that some took this as a sign of man's ingratitude to women; they loved their missionary sewing, and some were naturally inclined to switch all their needles to Kaffraria. But that sad happening may well have been the beginning of the great CWMA annual Chanda Sale. Well done, CWMA!

Chanda never girned about lack of support. It got on with the job, and made do with what was available in cash and men and women. Some who knew India well maintained that Chanda put to very good use indeed the resources it received. And there was other support that was never lacking – that of prayer in Scotland. There perhaps Chanda had the edge: there were fewer known people to pray for, and most had Scottish connections. Whatever the reason, I think we all felt this help, and valued it. In this connection, I must pay tribute to the work of Miss Marion Millar, who for very many years made up and sent out the little Chanda prayer leaflet. Now that Indians from Chanda come to Scotland from time to time for study, Episcopalians have the chance of continuing this helpful work of prayer for particular people. And they are all missionaries still. Today, such visitors are usually financed by other Scottish partners of the United Church of North India.

Elsewhere in this book, it will be evident what encouragement it gives and what a welcome they get when Episcopalians visiting India look in on their Christian brothers and sisters in Chanda and in Nagpur. They are assured of a most generous welcome. Nagpur is in the centre of India, with excellent air and rail connections.

Bishop Alex. Wood

THE BISHOPS OF NAGPUR

Bishop Copleston was Metropolitan in Calcutta when Christians first started evangelism in Chanda, and was therefore Chanda's first Bishop. To his honour he managed to get to Chanda to lay the foundation stone of St Andrew's Church in 1902.

Thereafter, in 1903, the Diocese of Nagpur was carved out of the Diocese of Calcutta. The new diocese covered most of the centre of India, and had an area nearly seven times that of England. Bishop Copleston averred that "two-thirds of the romance of Indian history lies in the Diocese." The man chosen to be Bishop was Eyre Chatterton, and Chanda was fortunate in him since he had been head of the Dublin University Mission at Hazaribagh. Alex Wood had called in there when he first came to Chanda. The first official visit of the episcopate was to Chanda in 1903, where he found the plague raging. Towards the end of the year the Bishop returned to consecrate the new church on St Andrew's Day.

In 1919, Foss Wescott, the Bishop of Chota Nagpur, moved to Calcutta as Metropolitan. (Chota admittedly means small, but the Diocese of Chota Nagpur lies some 400 miles to the NE of Nagpur. In area it is a small diocese, in the numbers of Christians it is vastly bigger than Nagpur, since there was a mass movement there under German missionaries in the middle of the 19th century, and again in the 1920s). When Foss Wescott moved it was not very surprising that he asked Canon Alex Wood to be his successor in Chota Nagpur.

Since Bishop Wood was to return to Chanda, and often appears in this book, I may perhaps be forgiven for telling one of his favourite stories. It will certainly revive memories for any who have been in India: A certain Mrs Halifax was keen on making a new garden. Her husband was the DC – District Commissioner and senior magistrate. Mrs Halifax had told her bearer to find a gang of men to work on the garden. Next day she noticed a crowd of men sitting about in the garden. Shocked, she turned to the bearer, and burst out in her best Hindi or Marathi: "Come on ... get a move on... put them to work... hurry up!" The servant demurred and, with a good deal of chivvying, obeyed. When the Memsahib was satisfied, the bearer went to find his master.

"Sahib, no doubt the Memsahib is right in putting all these people to work, but in fact they are the witnesses for the prosecution in the case you are to hear this morning."

Bishop Chatterton, the Bishop of Nagpur, retired in 1926. Again, it was natural for Foss Wescott the Metropolitan, to ask Alex Wood to move to Nagpur. Nagpur was vastly greater than Chota Nagpur in area, probably more difficult to administer, and it had several important military centres. The Christians of Chanda and the people in general were overjoyed to have their old friend back as Bishop. During his last furlough in Scotland the Bishop looked in at Forfar, where he had been curate, and on the Coplands there, and had met Cuthbert Hall at St. Margaret's, Newlands in Glasgow. Bishop Wood died in Shanghai, while taking a message of greeting from the Church of India to the Church of Japan.

Bishop Wood's mantle may not have fallen on my shoulders completely, but I was given his down sleeping-bag – though it was only once used in Chanda.

The story repeats itself. The head of the Dublin University Mission at Hazaribagh was chosen to be the new Bishop of Nagpur. Alex Hardy and his wife, herself a missionary doctor, proved to be great friends and guides to the Chanda missionaries and the Indian staff. Always there was a friendly welcome at Bishop's House, and advice and encouragement when needed. Bishop Hardy saw us through the war to Independence, under him the diocensanization of the parishes went forward, and we got an Indian majority on the Mission Managing Committee. Perhaps the latter did not mean very much at the time, since every one deferred to the Bishop's authority and missionary experience.

Bishop Hardy's retirement in 1947, called for what I think was the first election of a Bishop of Nagpur. In 1944 the General Council of the Church of India, Burma and Ceylon had appealed to dioceses to elect Indian bishops. In Nagpur several names were put forward. I think I proposed Archdeacon Chelvam, one of our senior priests. Canon Sinker's name was also put forward. He had been headmaster of Bishop Cotton School in Simla, and for the last two years secretary of the Bible Society stationed in Nagpur. At the time of the election, Canon Sinker was in England. The Archdeacon came at the top of the poll, and the Canon very low down. But no one had enough votes to be elected, and by the Diocesan constitution the appointment lapsed to the Archbishop of Canterbury. Canon Sinker was appointed, and on his return from England was consecrated in Nagpur on Candlemas, 1949.

During Bishop Sinker's episcopate the Diocese relinquished the lovely bungalow on the hill, and the Bishop wisely moved into Cathedral House.

Bishop Sinker resigned in 1954, and was succeeded by the first Indian Bishop of Nagpur, Sadanand Pathak. There was much rejoicing at having an Indian as Bishop, but his episcopate was to be sadly short. In Chanda the Revd George Wells was Head from 1953, and Bishop Pathak made him Archdeacon of Nagpur. The Bishop died after an operation, in May 1957. Bishop Sadiq wrote of him: "My Anglican orthodoxy was already suspect. Bishop S A Pathak, who was the first Indian Bishop of Nagpur, was a good biblical scholar, a good pastor and very much devoted to his family. He was, however, zealous in maintaining the Anglican position and not very enthusiastic about inter-church relations."

John Sadiq was consecrated in Pune (Poona) on 15th September, 1957, to be Bishop of Nagpur. Rather happily, there was consecrated with him a former Chanda boy, one of the first to go to the university at Hislop College, the Presbyterian college in Nagpur. The Chanda boy was Arthur Luther, consecrated to be Bishop of Nasik, and later moving to Bombay. The Diocese must have changed its method of election of bishops, since Sadiq tells us he was appointed by the Metropolitan and two other bishops who had been named by the Diocese. The Bishop was installed in his Cathedral by Archdeacon George Wells.

Bishop Sadiq figures rather prominently here, since he has left us his autobiography. He came of Muslim stock, was on the staff of the National Christian Council in Nagpur, and was ordained at the invitation of Bishop Sinker. He says he was not deeply Anglican and that his children were baptised by a Presbyterian friend. He tells us he never had a pastoral charge. Of his ordination, Bishop Sadiq records that the Revd Wm Stewart, a Presbyterian missionary in Nagpur, and an old friend of Chanda missionaries, was by Bishop Sinker asked to preach. "This raised a storm in the minds of one or two missionaries of the Episcopal Church of Scotland". The one or two must have been the Venerable G R Wells and the Revd J K Towers; Copland was on furlough. "A complaint was made to the Metropolitan and George (Sinker) was reprimanded." The preachment must have been contrary to the Indian Canons.

His references to Chanda seem a little naive. "The Christian community being largely from an economically backward class and in fact descendants of a few families saved from a severe famine ... treated with unwise generosity." 250-300 orphans hardly add up to a few families. Today, Bob Geldoff would approve of trying to keep the orphans alive. The Bishop may have forgotten that his own father was given mission work after his baptism. The Bishop's remark about generosity is quite in fashion about spoon-feeding and often there cannot help being some truth in it. Probably he had not heard of the Kabir Panthis at the beginning of the century, or of the influx of village catechumens in 1926 and 1936.

In 1958 at Lambeth, the new Bishop made his "maiden speech on the urgent need for unity on the score of the Churches' credibility and missionary effectiveness." Anyone who says that is in good company, and anyone who reads the Bible knows that our divisions are sinful. Yet in the face of Hinduism, at least, our sinful divisions are not quite so damning or so hindering as may be supposed: Christians can intermarry, and can eat together. Hindus cannot. "My second and last speech was a plea for total rejection of war, and it was a cry in the wilderness."

Bishop Sadiq also enjoyed being an observer at the Vatican Council. But that was only one of his many extra-diocesan and international commitments. As his episcopate drew to a close, he must have qualified for a book of records, by reason of the number of committees on which he served.

In Bishop Sadiq's time, the diocesanization of the Mission was completed. It meant little change, but rather putting into writing what was already established. In 1946 St Thomas had been given a small endowment and handed over to the Diocese. St Andrew's had followed suit. The Managing Committee already had an Indian majority. In war time it was accepted that a missionary would go wherever the Bishop wanted him. The big change under Bishop Sadiq was the legal transfer of the remaining land and buildings to the Diocese.

In the cold weather of 1970 Bishop Sadiq played host to the many who came to Nagpur for the inauguration of the United Church of North India. To him, that was a triumph and a very great joy, as it was to so many. With the inauguration of the United Church, Sadiq resigned, to make way for new blood.

The new Bishop, the first Bishop of Nagpur in the United Church, was the Rt Revd G Bhandare. Our then Primus and the Halls and the Coplands met him before his consecration, at the centenary celebrations for Christianity in Chanda and Nagpur. He was, I think, of Methodist stock, and he impressed us as being keen to learn what a bishop should be. It was, of course, a great joy to know that Chandrapur now had a Marathi speaker as well as an Indian for a Bishop. Later, the Bishop became assistant Moderator of the Church.

Bishop Bhandare resigned, and the next Bishop was Vinod Peter. His coming added joy on joy for Chandrapur Christians: he was an Indian, a Marathi speaker, and a Chanda boy. In fact, he was from

Bhadrawati, sixteen miles north west of Chandrapur. His father was an independent tekidar or small contractor, and his charming mother is still alive. The Bishop's wife, Rachel bai, was the daughter of one of Chanda's leading priests, the late Habel Jagtap. He, it was, who is recorded as having preached a most moving sermon at the requiem in St Thomas', Nagpur, for Canon Philip. The Bishop was a graduate of Hislop College, the college of our Presbyterian friends in Nagpur. Then he went to Bishop's College in Calcutta. He was rector of St Thomas' in Nagpur before going to Bombay. And he had already visited Scotland. We would do well to support him regularly with our prayers.

Bishop Hardy,
Revd. C. M. Copland and
Revd. R. H. C. Hall

THE LADIES OF THE MISSION

The ladies from very early days have set a magnificent example of good service and of generously long service. Miss Smyth and Mrs Aitken came in 1902. Miss Smyth later became Mrs Philip. In time, she and her husband moved to Nagpur and became the inspiration of St Thomas' Church and congregation there from 1909. Mrs Philip began what was to grow into All Saints Hostel for Girls. Sometime after her husband's death in 1925, Mrs Philip moved to Jabalpur. During the war she came to the rescue of the Mission by letting us have her open tourer Austin Seven, and by letting us have it at the government and not the market price. Canon Philip's sister was a well-known member of the congregation in Cults, his brother a much loved rector in Kirriemuir for close on thirty years.

Biblewomen setting out

Miss Rowell joined the Mission in 1903, and gave almost twenty years of selfless service, leaving in 1922. We can tell little of her today, but it is known that she was well loved and that she loved Chanda. Miss Rowell gave me her Marathi Prayer Book in 1938.

In 1917, Miss Woodcock arrived and she was followed by Miss Flint in 1919. These two led the women's work nobly for two decades. Miss Woodcock was in charge of the girls' hostel and the girls' middle school and primary school in Chanda. Miss Flint concentrated on the evangelistic side with the Biblewomen. Miss Woodcock left the impression of being tough, Miss Flint of being gentle. Both were firm, very greatly loved and respected. In the '30s Manorama bai Rao was head of the middle school, Dya bai Moon head of the primary. Monica bai Luther was in charge of the girls' hostel, later being succeeded by

Martha bai Fegrade. Again in the '30s and beyond, Satyawati bai was the chief Biblewoman, aided by Nirmala bai Kurne and others. They were indefatigable in visiting, teaching and preaching in the nearby villages, or in camping at the more distant ones when the men had established contact.

The Women's Hospital

For the women's hospital, the record is not so complete. Miss Ungate came in 1922, Dr Ward in 1926, Miss Ivy McLeod soon afterwards. Towards the end of the '30s, Sharada bai was the head nurse, a tall figure who was delightfully dependable. During the war we had Dr Stillwell from Australia, and then Dr Pratapsingh from Hazaribagh, trained at Ludiana. In her retirement, Dr Pratapsingh lived with the Wantage Sisters in Pune. Later Dr Kashyap took over.

Miss M K Booth joined the Mission in 1932, mainly for educational work. Special tribute should be paid to her mother, who braved the trying climate of Chanda and came to join Miss Booth so that she could continue her work.

Miss Booth recalls a rare experience at Junona, when they were frightened by a tiger growling. They all clambered up some trees, though I doubt if they got up the recommended fifteen feet! Miss Booth had another adventure when she and Dr Peters and a senior nurse had been working at Mul, driven by Padre Armstrong. They had had no rain, but there must have been rain somewhere for the Andhari river had got up. On the way home the car got stuck on the middle of a low Irish bridge, with the water steadily rising. The Padre found he could not stand against the current. They sat tight. And the water came up. At last, some Hindu cartmen gathered on the opposite bank. The biggest of the men tried to swim to the car. Three times he was washed down stream. Finally, they tied a rope to the man. He got to the car and fixed the rope to it. With the help of the rope, he carried the ladies slung over his shoulder to the far bank. Later the car was recovered, and did further service. Miss Booth's first visit to Mul nearly proved her last. That Andhari river now has a hydro-electric dam in the middle of the jungle.

Sad to say, the Revd H F A Treble and Mrs Treble were caught in a similar flash flood in South Africa, when he had been invalided out of India, and they were both drowned.

Ultimately, Miss Booth and her mother had to leave for health reasons in 1941. That left the women's side bereft, and it brought back Miss Flint who had retired to Kenya the previous year. It brought, too, a generous offer of help from Miss Molly Mackenzie. Miss Mackenzie's home had been in Chanda when her parents were there. She had lived in Chanda 1938-9, and was already well known and liked by all – by the Indian government officials and their wives as well as by the Christians. In the end she got to Chanda by convoy to Panama, and then via New Zealand, where she worked her passage picking peas. Miss Flint and Miss Mackenzie held the fort for the remainder of the war. In 1945 Miss Mackenzie and the Revd Cuthbert Hall were married, and in 1948, to the sorrow of all, they moved to Nasik Diocese. Of course, they kept up their Chanda connections.

In 1943 the Mission sent our first two girls to Nagpur University, in the care of our Presbyterian friends at Hislop College. Many trained for nursing at their Mure Hospital in Nagpur, several went for teacher's training at Pune, with the Wantage Sisters, and one, I think, took higher nursing training in Delhi.

Thereafter, it was the married women who carried most of the burden. After the Halls left in 1948, Mrs Copland stood in; Miss Helen Wells (Sister of the Revd G R Wells) joined the Mission in 1947, and became Mrs John Towers in 1948. In 1950 the Revd G R Wells married Miss Ann Maclellan, who was one of the Presbyterian missionaries in Pune. Mrs Wells was very fully equipped to help in Chandrapur: she already had Marathi, and was a trained educationalist, a blessing to Chanda.

Miss E Holmes joined the Mission in 1946. Miss Holmes had been second in command of education in the whole of the Central Provinces. She had lately been awarded the MBE. I remember walking through the marble halls of the Secretariat building to visit her by appointment in her spacious cool office in Nagpur. There was a flunkey at the door, with a gold puggaree and a dagger in his belt. I found a little lady with grey hair, sitting at a huge desk at the far side of the room, under a twirling fan. I don't know if I got what I wanted then. But when she retired, Miss Holmes joined us. With her wide experience and qualifications, Miss Holmes was a great help and her gentleness made her loved by all.

Miss Peggy Weetman joined the hospital staff in 1952. She was followed by Miss Eleanor Williams, 1953-57. Neither was able to stay long, but their help was most welcome. There followed Miss Dorothea Ward in 1962, coming under the auspices of the USPG, and leaving in 1970. In 1986, Miss Anne Thomson from Christ Church, Morningside, volunteered to help. Anne arrived in the aftermath of great floods and was flung into distributing relief to the homeless.

Now, Hislop College has come to Chandrapur! For years the Mission has been sending young men and women to the College in Nagpur, part of the Nagpur University, and run by those who were our Presbyterian friends and are now fellow members of the United Church of North India. On 4th August, 1986 a foundation stone was laid, and classes for girls started. "Teaching will be on science, leading to agriculture."

A MISSIONARY ON TOUR

Extracts from a letter from Miss Molly Mackenzie

KAPSI REST HOUSE – I was interrupted yesterday by the visit of a little Sikh girl, the daughter of the Vihad forest ranger, begging me to go to her house. Satiwati Bai (Biblewoman) and I went and got a great welcome, although the man was in bed with fever. They were Punjabis from near Delhi, and the woman was delighted when I managed to speak to her in Urdu (Hindustani). I came out here a week ago. Satiwati Bai, Nirmalla, Daji (cook) and I set out to Mul by 'bus. I stayed a night there in the Dak Bungalow. Bajerao, the Catechist, and family live in the Mission Rest House there now. The next day I set off on my cycle with Bajerao Master and we visited two villages on the way to Saoli, while the women followed with the saman (baggage) in a bullock cart. Daji cycled on ahead, and had a most welcome lunch ready for me when I arrived. There is a dear little bungalow at Saoli just outside the village. We had two nights there visiting in Saoli itself and some of the villages round.

We then went on to Vihad. Another nice bungalow, but right in the village. Ayah's husband, John, is the Khansamah (cook in charge) there. Mr Copland arrived in Saoli after we left to do a tour with Bajerao to the south of us. The first day in Vihad was Sunday, so he cycled over about 7.30 from Soali to give us Holy Communion. We had a good service, the two Bais, our Christian gadiwala (cartman), Mr Copland's servant, and John the Khansamah. After three nights in Vihad we came on here this morning.

Kapsi is right in the jungle, and the little rest house where I am staying has the jungle right up to its doorstep. We are just outside the village, and it is most attractive. I walked here with Nirmalla, taking another village on the way, about eight miles. Daji brought my bike. There are a series of canals all round this part from Assolamenda Tank, and it is lovely cycling along the canal paths, though decidedly tricky. I am just loving this tour, it has all gone so easily.

Evangelistic camp

The people round here seem really interested and most friendly, the caste folk as well as the Mahars. In several villages they openly asked about Baptism etc. The last few years this district has had a good deal of attention. Bajerao at Mul is really a great success and seems really liked in the district. In both Vihad and Kapsi they are asking for a school. We shall supply the master when they have built the school and master's house. It would be a great thing to have a good Christian family in some of these villages.

I have another week here, and then return to Chanda in time for our Staff retreat, which Canon Streatfeild is conducting. After that I am going out again, to Sakerwai this time, following Mr Hall and the Catechists, who are there now. Agnes and Louisa (Biblewomen) are to be with me. It is tents of course at Sakerwai.

Must stop now and have a bath and dinner. Chicken to-night, a great treat. John at Vihad got it for me. Otherwise it is dal (lentils) and rice. The bread is finished too, of course, but Daji makes very good little chapattis. I have managed to get eggs too, which are a great stand-by.

CRISIS

When Hall and I got to Chanda in the autumn of 1938, we soon learnt to expect a crisis every six months or so, whereas in the Church in Scotland we supposed there might possibly be one in ten years. Clearly, that was a long time ago.

The first was probably the greatest. Alex Wood was plunged into a great famine almost as soon as he arrived. Then he had his 250-300 children, to try and keep them alive, to bury the dead and feed and teach and train the survivors. Of that time a tale is told. It must have been known that Wood was disbursing government money for the road works. Once when he returned home, he found a Pathan gently roasting some part of the mission clerk, to encourage him to hand over the safe key. Wood went for him like a tiger. The Pathan was a marked man in more ways than one, and he was never seen again. We never quite equalled that.

Our crises were minor at first. The Bishop of Nasik, Philip Lloyd, later of St Albans, was very kind to Cuthbert Hall and me, and we used to stay with him going to and from the language school – a most excellent institution – at Mahableshwar beyond Poona. The Bishop was away, and Cuthbert went down with fever. He had a most useful book on tropical medicine: malaria seemed too simple, cholera seemed unlikely since he was still alive, typhoid was the answer. All the same, a dose or two of quinine did the trick, and I don't think we referred to the book again.

It may have been on the same visit that the Bishop asked me to deputize for an Indian parish priest somewhere, while the priest came in to Nasik for an ordination. It was a CMS parish, and Trinity Sunday coming up. I thought I knew about the Communion service but wanted to get the details of Matins straight.

"Do you use the full exhortation?"

"We have wafers here, I hope you don't mind."

"How about the Creed, do you use the Athanasian Creed?"

"It is our custom to use wine here."

"OK by me: is not that what our Lord used?"

"I hope you don't mind, we have the one cup here."

"That is just what I am accustomed to: isn't it a wonderful demonstration of fellowship, and particularly in India!"

It took time to dawn on me that this simple old Indian priest was, in spite of the Bishop's recommendation, wanting to make sure that I really was a priest, before letting me loose on his parish. Living near Bombay he must have absorbed the Scottish heresy, that all good Scots are Presbyterians!

Quite early on I was sent to Nagpur to learn the ropes of St. Thomas' and the lie of the land. The Marrisons of the Church Army very kindly took me in. The church was then rather a drab building, red brick inside and out, though magnificent in size and layout. It was built by the inspiration of Canon Philip. The church was designed by a Mr Lloyd of the Oxford Mission to Calcutta. In 1926 the Primus (Bishop Robberds) assisted on St Thomas' Day (then 21st December) at the consecration of the church. He was accompanied on his visit to India by Mrs Robberds, who later became an aunt of Mrs C M Copland. With them was "the Secretary Saheb", the Revd H McNaught, that doughty warrior for missions (of Lockerbie, Maryhill and Pitlochry). Recently the Diocese was given a chalice which had belonged to Bishop Robberds. In later years Mrs Robberds laughingly recalled her shock in Chanda at seeing a row of toads in her bathroom watching her ablutions. She might have been frightened had she known that toads (or is it only frogs?) make a tasty bit for snakes.

Soon after I got to Nagpur, Mr Treble went down with typhoid, and I was recalled to Chanda, I suppose to make company for Hall or to hold the safe key while the clerk, the admirable Ruben Master, guided the Mission finances.

I think it must have been in my first rains that I got something like dysentery, and was sent to be vetted in the big government hospital in Nagpur. There I met Molly Mackenzie, literally carrying round a boy more than half her size. His foot had been poisoned by a dusty spike at the foot of a date palm, and had not responded to treatment in Chanda. (We had no antibiotics then.) She was trying to get him attended to in the hospital, where later his lower leg was amputated. The Revd Anand Michael became known to many in Scotland.

An even more striking amputation tale is told of Dr Mackenzie. On both occasions when he was in Chanda, he came as a priest rather than as a doctor, but there was a school master whose leg obviously needed to come off. There was no one else to do it, so Dr Mackenzie did the job, to the lasting praise of the nurses and the blessings of Thomas Ghadge, whose family later played leading parts in the Christian communities of Chandrapur and Nagpur.

Early on, Cuthbert Hall ran a slow pulse or something like that, and was to be sent up to Bangalore to recuperate and I was to go to take care of him on the journey. Bangalore sounded good. Alas, Cuthbert improved, and went on his own!

Manohar's young wife had a swelling on her right wrist. The Mure hospital in Nagpur had advised amputation. My wife had trained at the Royal Free in London, and was naturally inclined to heed medical opinion, but she and Vishranti were loath to part with the hand. So Vishranti was sent to Bombay for a second opinion. It was the same. The two women determinedly held out, and Vishranti had the use of her hand. It was not until much later that at last the hand had to go. Not many people can have been glad to be on a hospital waiting list for forty years!

Leprosy was quite a scourge, though it is not noticeable in its early stages. I remember we were once told that the Mul area had a higher incidence of leprosy than most other parts of India. Verrier Elwin, who was persona grata at Government House, and not surprisingly in his particular case persona non grata with Bishop Wood, in one of his books had a sad story of a Gond lad idly watching an ant crawl up his leg. Suddenly he realised he no longer felt it: that was the beginning of leprosy. (Bishop Luther when he retired from Bombay became Secretary of the Indian Leprosy Mission).

Malaria was our obvious scourge, but we were well trained: nets at night, and in the evening long trousers, long boots, and long sleeves, while the ladies took refuge – or rather their feet did – in pillowslips. Quinine was unobtainable at one time during the war, then came paludrin and later metacrin. I still have writ large in an English Prayer Book (only for the daily psalms) the word "CHARITRA", a leaf we were to ask for if ever we were caught out in a village without quinine. Malaria, and unboiled water: I am sure to this day we owe a tremendous debt to our servants, Christian, Hindu and Muslim, who kept the rule of giving us in the jungle, in the villages or at home, only boiled water. The European missionaries thank and honour them all for that safe kindness!

Greville Williamson buried at Kohima. Wendy's brother.

We did not often get malaria, but soon after she arrived in Chanda, my wife got rather a fright. I went down with fever in some village. We could not have had the driver with us, for she had to motor me home. Dr Pratapsingh, our lady doctor, naturally started treating a temperature as malaria, and if the patient did not respond she moved on to treatment for typhoid. I got the typhoid treatment. This was the only time I got a bit delirious: I was on the point of solving some abstruse mathematical problem, but never quite made it. My wife's two brothers had died in India during the war and she had young aunts and uncles buried at the CMS Mission at Mundla in our diocese. She wondered if the time had come to tell my family in Britain. Mrs Hardy, our Bishop's wife, was a doctor, and when consulted advised delay. The patient recovered, perhaps from sandfly fever.

The mathematical problem reminds me of a somewhat similar crisis when Dr Mackenzie was trying me out, to see if I could drive a car. It was an open tourer, an Austin, I think. I asked what pace I should go. "Anything up to 30." I wanted to prove my worth and tried to get the needle up to 30, but every time it got to 28 or 29 it slipped back, and I had to keep on trying. I had noticed that when Dr Mackenzie was driving, he would take a hand off the wheel and point to a village here, or a tank there, whereas I would not have dared doing such a thing. I put it down to my inexperience. Then we came to a river crossing and I had to stop. A quiet voice came over my shoulder: "I am sorry: I forgot to tell you that the speedometer doesn't work." An audible sigh of relief went up all round.

During the war there were various flaps. Naturally there were all sorts of Diocesan plans suggested for us and shelved. The Bishop wanted one of us to go to the north of the Diocese towards Delhi. Of course he would go. Even after the war, strange thoughts could crop up. I remember being asked to go from Forfar to meet the Convener of the Mission Board at Bishop's House in Glasgow. The CMS were drawing in their horns: they wondered if we could take on one of their missions about 450 miles away. I doubted if my journey was necessary, but went. We had our discussion, and at ten to one I was thanked and left the house. I wondered where I would get lunch, and found a most warm welcome in the tropical house of the Botanic Gardens, and there finished my breakfast sandwiches.

We had our own genuine local excitements. I suppose it was after Mr Ghandi's arrest that near Warora some twenty-eight miles to the north, the people got out of hand and three government officers were burnt to death. They happened to be a Christian, a Parsee, and a Muslim. Noticeably, none was a Hindu. One of us went there two days later with a brother of the Christian, to see what we could do. There was nothing and we concluded that the Parsees had more need of some bones than the rest of us. It was astounding how quickly things could boil up, and then calm down.

The same sort of thing happened in a minor key in Chanda. On the day that Mr Ghandi was imprisoned, the school children took to the streets. This was a new phenomenon. "All schools must close!" A great crowd of high school children surged down the drive into the women's compound. Cuthbert Hall stood sentry with his cycle ready to go to the police lines, though we realised that they would be fully occupied elsewhere. I went over to the ladies' bungalow to meet our visitors. On the front veranda I found myself supported by a tall fine-looking teacher, Grace bai Chotto, and – I thought surprisingly – by a simple Hindu whose field was behind the bungalow. He was leaning on his lathi, a big bamboo stick. The leader of the crowd turned out to be Wellinker, the brother of one of our outstanding catechists. That he should be leader I took as a tribute to Christian teaching and training.

"Sahib, you must close the school, or we will burn down all the buildings."

There was a good deal of talking and shouting back and forth. Grace bai tended to keep things in order. Finally I said, "You know this is the women's compound: you should not be here. If you go back out of the compound, I will close the school."

Then the grumbling began. "We don't know if the Sahib will do what he says ..."

That brought in Grace bai. "Wellinker, you ought to be ashamed: you know perfectly well that the Sahib will do what he says."

So the agreement was made, and I strolled with them down the 200 yards or so of the drive, chatting about their exams, asking when they would be sitting matric and so on. Happily, all was peace. To this day, I have never asked what happened at the boys' school of the Mission within the city walls. But the schools were not burnt. The headmasters must have had wisdom as great as mine! Wellinker became a pillar of church and of society.

At that difficult time, the Mission ladies gave shelter to the wife of an Indian government officer who was out in the district. He thought the ladies' bungalow would be the last to be burnt. Hindu or Muslim, I don't know.

One crisis I could have brought on myself. In the hot weather of these troublous times I remember pushing away some villager who was pestering me for something. Then suddenly I remembered that a week or two before, one of our most distinguished Bishops in the south had been forced to resign and return to Britain: he had struck a teacher, and had been convicted in the court. I confess I had one or two sleepless nights. I had certainly touched the villager, which was not customary. A newspaper headline could have turned that into a ferocious attack, and an astute lawyer could have done the rest. I was relieved in a day or two when it was clear that all was forgotten and forgiven, or more probably that my "assault" had never been noticed by a kindly villager.

Around the time of Mr Ghandi's arrest, Bishop Hardy happened to be with us for meetings. A local Christian pleader (lawyer) took the opportunity to attack the Head of the Mission. Very properly, the Bishop gave him a long and patient hearing. The Head survived.

That same evening, the head Biblewoman, Satyawati bai, came over to us and quietly said that the young people among the Christians were going to lock the Bishop out of St Andrew's church next morning. Instead of going about 6.30, the Bishop and Cuthbert Hall and I went down about 6.00. I had a short crowbar under my cassock. But it was not needed: we had got there first. And to their honour, the young people when they arrived came in and joined in the Eucharist.

It may well have been that same morning, we were told of trouble brewing in the boys' hostel. So the hostel was closed while the boys were at school. When they returned, boys from villages outside Chanda were given their fares home. Thereafter, I made an intensive study of the government education manual. Within a fortnight, the hostel was reopened as a "home boarding", giving us rather more authority than previously. All was well.

In those days of naturally fierce nationalist feeling, whether with curates or school children or in the country at large, Scottish history had given us considerable sympathy and understanding of the clamour. We remembered that Edward I's firm and efficient English rule was never quite accepted as a substitute for home rule in Scotland.

When she came to Chanda, Miss Peggy Weetman, a nurse, went in at the deep end. We had gone to Kapsi, some ten miles off any road. In the evening, a distraught husband arrived from a village five miles away. We knew nothing of them, but they had heard of us. He had come in what I suppose could be described as a racing bullock cart – a ringi, very much a single seater. He had heard we had a nurse: would she please come and help his wife, who was in difficulty in childbirth. Peggy was magnificent. She took her bag and not much else, got up astride the ringi sitting pillion behind the driver, and so set off into the dark with a man we had never met before, to an unknown village, without a word of their language. The baby arrived. And Peggy returned.

Ordinarily, when cholera was in the offing, all the world was offered injections in the police lines. It had struck badly in 1924 when Dr Wellington, Miss Brechin, and the nurses made a name for themselves, and gave more than 2,000 injections. It struck again heavily in Peggy

Weetman's time. Things in the city were pretty bad. Peggy Weetman and Eleanor Williams and their nurses took over the town hall, and did a very fine job. Sad to say, the son of one of our nurses, Ruth bai, caught the cholera, and died. He was the only son of his mother, and she was a widow.

Peggy Weetman

WAR AND PEACE

During the war, in Chanda and in the district I think we were accepted and never molested. After all, the Mission was very much part of the local scene. When we went back in 1970, after some eighteen years, as I was walking to church about 6.30 in the morning, an old man called out "Saheb, quotoun ala?" – "Where have you been?" In Nagpur one did hear shouts of "British go home!" This, I think, was particularly at the time of Sir Stafford Cripps' visit. At that time I remember being on the station platform at Nagpur, when Mr Ghandi arrived to the welcome of a great crowd. In Delhi, Mr Treble suffered for wearing khaki, when he was hit on the head by a running mob. Possibly Hall and I were favoured by adopting a white cassock for general wear. Once, when changing trains in Delhi, I was accosted by a very vociferous guard, in a language unknown. I thought he was going to hand me over to the police for some offence against war regulations. When he left, I quickly changed my coach. But he came back and found me, and to my surprise brought me a tray of tea. He was a welcoming fellow Christian.

"The Revd C M Copland is leaving the Mission to become a chaplain." This, a report to the Overseas Mission Board in Edinburgh in November 1940. It was nearly, but not quite, true. It was part of a complicated story. When I came down from Cambridge I belonged to the Reserve of Officers. At Cambridge I was a Bombardier in the OTC. The gunners of the OTC had horses! Some time before Munich, more than a year before Cuthbert Hall and I went to India, the Scottish Bishops had agreed that if there was war I could go as chaplain. When war came, India did not need any chaplains. Later, we met the Chaplain General at Bishop's House in Nagpur, and it was arranged that Copland should go. (I still have the khaki stockings bought then. In the Mission we avoided stockings like the plague, on account of spear grass sticking in them and attacking one's legs.) Then Mr Treble was hit on the head in Delhi, and had to leave us. Bishop Hardy said Copland must stay. And that was that.

During the war, there was naturally much chopping and changing of plans. Scotland thought the Australian Board of Missions might help us, particularly on the ladies' side. Then it was to be an American Sisterhood. Bishop Hardy spoke of Siamese Sisters (I may have got the country wrong) who had to go somewhere. Bishop Appleton had got out of Rangoon: he might come and join us.

In the end we only had passing visitors, though always welcome. Corporal Miles of Forfar and the Black Watch, from the Chindits; men of the RAF who came to dismantle a Spitfire which had come down next to the Mission. (They built an effective open-air oven at the ladies' bungalow.) Another RAF visitor looked in after the war; he was from Glasgow. The Revd Leslie Pennell stayed with us twice, and the Revd R C Hastie-Smith joined us in a retreat in Nagpur (Hastie's connections: Glenalmond, Aboyne, Forfar, Strathtay).

From time to time we had interesting encounters on the train. Once, when I had the Diocesan first-class pass, I jumped into a compartment and found a Roman Catholic priest just beginning his lonely Mass. He was glad for me to serve. One Good Friday I found a whole train load of Italian prisoners stopped in Chanda station. I had on a white cassock; I had a cross; I greeted them, and did what I could for them in French that kept breaking into Marathi. At least they were reminded that it was Good Friday.

When it seemed that the Japanese were coming, Cuthbert Hall and I had our plans. We would retire into the jungle among the Gonds with Canon Patwardhan, taking with us explosives from one of the collieries. Sometimes we would slip out and minister to the faithful in the villages, and at other times we could give our attention to blowing up the main line between Delhi and Madras. Probably neither plan would have worked for long. Perhaps we had not worked out the question of being combatants or non-combatants. At least Cuthbert Hall had the advantage of being dark enough to be taken for an Indian.

Even in India we had some rationing – of petrol, and kerosene, and sugar, and cloth. It was a compliment to Prabhudas Chandekar, our headmaster at the new Vihad school, that he was appointed government rationing officer there. As mentioned elsewhere, cement was rationed, too.

To help the Christian community with soaring prices we laid in a store of rice and jewari during the harvest. It was stored in the open, near our bungalow, with only a roof over it, yet we did not suffer from human or rodent pilfering. Ruben Master, the mission clerk, with the help of the Biblewomen, did most of the buying. They were very particular, and critical of what was offered. It was all quite entertaining, though of course, responsible work.

Around 1941 or 1942, when men in khaki appeared on the trains, or even in the villages, we had to tell the people to be friends with them. Some forty or so Christians from Chanda joined up. Later we heard well of a Chanda man in the Sudan. Some served with Pye Force in Syria. Of those who were taken prisoner by the Japanese, it was notable that none of them joined the Indian Independence Army raised by the Japanese, in spite of the inducements offered.

To quote from a letter by the Revd W B Currie, later Provost of the Cathedral in Perth, in **The Scottish Guardian** of 18th January, 1946: "In the spring of 1942 I was stationed as Chaplain with a military hospital in the Sudan near the village of Gebeit in the Red Sea hills, with an Indian military hospital attached to us. At my first celebration of the Holy Communion there I found in the congregation an Indian Lance-Corporal who gave his name as Peter. What was most interesting was that he came from Chanda. It was wonderful to meet the fruits of our Chanda Mission out there in that lonely desert post. Lance-corporal Peter was one of my most faithful communicants. He never missed a Sunday Communion when it was at all possible to attend, and this says a great deal as Peter was a cook, and of all the duties in the Army that is the most difficult as regards obtaining free time. It was difficult to be free even for 6.30 a.m., which was the hour of the celebration. I only knew Peter for a short time before he was posted to another unit, but it was sufficient to give glorious testimony to the work of our Mission in Chanda."

Who was this Peter? Was it Peter who was a tailor in Chanda, and a brilliant hockey player? In Chanda he was distinguished as a man who had repeatedly been offered a place in the police – a coveted job – and had repeatedly turned the offer down. They wanted him for their hockey team, but he was reputed to feel that the police would be too much like hard work! He did not find worship too hard in the Sudan.

INDEPENDENCE: 15TH AUGUST 1947

This was naturally a time for very great rejoicing. Overnight the Imperial Mail Service became the Indian Mail Service, and the letters IMS remained on the railway vans. And on them, the crown was easily changed to an Indian lion.

The government was not fanatical about getting rid of old things; even some of Queen Victoria's statues survived. At the time of partition, I have a feeling that people in Britain knew more of the slaughter than we did in the middle of India. At that time, some Christian nurses passed through Chanda from the south, going to minister to the wounded and mutilated in the Muslim-Hindu-Sikh holocaust. They knew that language would not protect them from attack, nor dress. They donned crosses, which was not their custom, to show who they were and what was their purpose. They survived.

After Independence, we rather expected that we might be pushed to the back of the queue in the post office and elsewhere. In fact, we still had to resist being pushed to the front. I remember mentioning to the DC – the senior government officer – that we would like to take some of the hostel children to a certain PWD bungalow, and that we did not feel like paying the full charge. "Oh, I'll tell the PWD" That might have done in the old days, but not now. "Please don't: but you might mention that you are glad to know we are applying."

The National Constitution guaranteed freedom to anyone to practise and to propagate their religion but it was a crime to "convert" anyone for reward. Some local states interpreted that rather strictly: if you did not win anyone with a dish of rice, you could still be accused of bribery by promising pie in the sky, or a place in heaven. Some Christians in other parts did suffer on that sort of charge. But the central government stood firm.

It is very much to the credit of all concerned that in the early years after Independence catechumens came forward in greater numbers than they did during the war years.

FRIENDSHIP

Mr Mitra had come to us from Bombay. He had been brought up by the Cowley Fathers, had served in the '14-'18 war, and is now a travelling Inspector on the railway. In this war several of his sons have joined the Navy, and one at least has worshipped with you in Scotland. The Mitras are stationed in Wardha. But we often see him in church and at breakfast in Chanda.

Mitra means friend, and to his name Mr. Mitra runs true. There is a delightful tale told of him during the exodus from Bombay. He had been sent there for special duty. Some of the Wantage Sisters were seeing off some Indian Sisters, going I think to Travancore. Enormous crowds swarmed at platform entrances, and only travellers were allowed on. Enter Mr. Mitra, and not yet on duty. "Good morning, Sisters." "Oh, Mr. Mitra, can you help us? There is this awful crowd and they won't let us on to the platform." "Well, I haven't reported for duty, but I'll see what I can do."

As it happened, beyond a bookstall was another gate on to the same platform. This was open. But the Sisters demurred: "Perhaps we aren't supposed to come in here?" "Oh, it's only a matter of convenience; there is a crowd there, and nobody here, so let us go."

So far so good. But the train was not only crammed, but overflowing with probably sixty or seventy people in a carriage for forty. What was to be done? Mr. Mitra spotted the Traffic Superintendent and went up to him: "Good morning, Sir. These Sisters are going to Travancore, and I find there is no Ladies Only on the train. Would you like me to label this for them?" "Most certainly. Turn these men out." So out of a smaller compartment meant for twenty at a pinch tumbled, at first with difficulty, and then with more obvious reluctance, some forty men. The label was put up, and the Sisters ensconced.

"Now, if you will excuse me, Sisters, I must report for duty." A friend indeed!

The Scottish Churchman.

The story of Mr Mitra is very like what happened to our daughter Jane when she and her future husband were visiting India in 1976.

In Chanda and in Nagpur they were treated like royalty. When leaving Nagpur, they got to the station about an hour before the train was due to leave. Mr Kamlaker Damle or someone exclaimed: "You really have not seen Nagpur!"

"But there is not much time: we don't want to miss the train to Calcutta."

"Oh, never mind: come on."

So off they were taken in a car, on a lightning tour of Nagpur.

Back at the station, they found a friendly crowd to see them off. In rolled the train, and they found themselves being shown into a first class coupe. "But we have booked into the second class." One of their friends, who turned out to be the assistant stationmaster, explained: "I know, but we have changed the reservation, as we thought this might be more comfortable." And Kamlaker, I think it was, or Bishop Luther, sent them off with the traditional Nagpur gift – a basket of their most delicious oranges.

REUNION

In the 1940s the Roman Catholics were far more forthcoming than they were in Britain. I remember travelling to Jabalpur one Maundy Thursday on a bus with some Roman Catholic nuns: they just treated me as a priest. That was to take a three hour service in Jabalpur. On the way, a peepul tree fell across our path, but we only ran into it gently, and someone had an axe handy.

In those days I imagine the National Christian Council had no Roman Catholics, and was largely Protestant. All the same, they accepted for their REVIEW an article I wrote on the prospects of reunion with Rome. I remember quoting a young priest – as he then was – Yvres Congar. And in writing the article, I was helped by a young priest of ours – Paul Yohan.

Then came the debates on the South India Scheme. In the Diocesan Council on one occasion Bishop Hardy mentioned the Roman Catholics, and a BCMS English priest said he wished they had never been mentioned. The Chanda clergy tended to criticize the Scheme: they were strongly in favour of reunion, but they felt the Scheme should be improved. We knew that Bishop Hardy was agonizing over the Scheme, but we did not know on which side he would come down. In 1944 when the final vote came in the Diocesan Council, Cuthbert Hall was there to record his vote, sitting on his luggage, as he was under orders to report to Deolali before going to Britain on a troopship. The voting was even. Bishop Hardy was against the Scheme as it was, and wanted it improved. Probably the main improvement sought was to have all clergymen Episcopally ordained from the beginning. The Bishop did not cast his vote so the Scheme was not passed by our Diocese, though the majority of the others approved it.

At some time towards the end of the thirty years or more taken in fashioning the Scheme for South India, the Scottish Bishops sent their considered opinion of the Scheme as it then was to the Metropolitan, for himself and the rest of the bishops of the Church of India, Burma and Ceylon.

Edinburgh told me of the document and even sent me a copy. The opinion was not altogether approving. I sent the document to our Bishop, or told him of its having been sent to Calcutta. He had heard nothing of it. Bishop Hardy jogged the elbow or the conscience of the Metropolitan, and the document was circulated.

Then came the decisive meeting of the General Council. It proved most interesting. It became clear that the motion to **approve** our four Southern Dioceses joining the United Church would not go through. I do not recollect the details: possibly it was the Bishops who would not approve. The wording was changed to **permit**. Bishop Hardy asked for time to consider what the change implied. Bishop Hollis of Madras, one of the chief supporters of the Scheme, generously agreed that that was proper. And all the time the Metropolitan was dealing out the voting papers. Permission was given.

Reunion came in 1947. I believe the arrangements worked extremely well, and today all ordinations are by bishops.

Anglicans were a majority in the south. In the north they were a minority. The later scheme for the north naturally benefited by experience with the south. In the north, from the first, ministries were united by Episcopal ordination or laying on of hands. (Rather amusingly, though no doubt some were sad about it, I think the Presbyterians in Madras and Bombay held out for a time: they were part of the Church of Scotland! And what lovely cool air-conditioned churches they had.)

The Halls and the Coplands, together with the Revd L E Luscombe, were in India in the autumn of 1970, for the centenary of the coming of Christianity to Chanda. We were in Nagpur only a few weeks before the inauguration there of the United Church of North India, and saw some of the preparations made for that great event. Mr Bhandare was to be the new Bishop of Nagpur. We met him, and rejoiced that Chandrapur would for the first time have an Indian Marathi-speaking bishop. Mr Bhandare was not an Anglican, but he gave the impression of being keen to learn what a bishop should be.

Mrs Copland, 1970, centenary of the mission

It is a great joy that Chanda's friends in Hislop College and in the Mure Hospital in Nagpur are now one with us and we with them in the United Church.

INSTITUTIONS

The hostels, and with them the schools and the hospital, are quite possibly the largely unsung and most effective and definite contribution to India through the years. In the early fifties, Indianisation was the great thing among missions and missionaries. It was about that time that a leading Indian Christian made an appeal in the NCC REVIEW. He held that the last work European missionaries should hand over must be their connection with children's hostels. He felt that the contribution in character-building in the hostels had been so great that it should be kept up as long as possible.

In Chanda, the ladies lived almost next door to the girls' hostel, and they made the best of their opportunities for informal as well as for formal contact. At language school in Mahableshwar, some of the first Marathi words we learnt were the adage "The hand that rocks the cradle rules the world." The Christian women knew the importance of the contribution they could make, and they were well content and generous in making it.

At the girls' hostel

The boys' hostel within the city walls was further away from the missionaries, but apart from formal visits there was a good deal of coming and going for games and swimming, and, of course, at the Christmas camps. As the hot weather came on, Cuthbert Hall and I used to cycle over the fields and join the hostel boys for swimming in the Erai river beyond the city wall. The water was pretty thick and reddish brown, but we were able to dive off the bank and it was all very refreshing. The boys benefited greatly from the parish priest living next door. In both hostels, the Indians in charge have always made a solid and reliable contribution to the general welfare.

From these hostels young men and women have gone for training as teachers and nurses to various government and mission colleges, in Delhi, Ratlam and Ahmednagar and Poona and elsewhere. Often they have passed out with distinction. Our special gratitude goes to our Scottish Presbyterian – as they then were – friends of Hislop College in Nagpur and of the Mure Memorial Hospital in that city. Priests have been trained in Bishop's College in Calcutta in English, and at Nasik in Marathi. Biblewomen and catechists have received their training in missionary colleges in the Marathi-speaking area. The first young women from the Mission went to Hislop College in 1943, less than ten years after our men had found their way there. Bishop Hardy used to stress how fortunate we were in not having any big institution to support, anchoring the Mission and its finances to a special location. That being so, we were all the more grateful for being allowed to benefit from other missions' colleges.

It was not easy to keep track of the good jobs Chanda men and women went into up and down the country. Several did well in government service, in the postal service, and in the railway. Members of St Thomas' congregation are mentioned elsewhere. David John became a lawyer in the railway in Bombay. Philip, an orphan, was in the Indian navy and visited Scotland on duty; later he was manager of a glass works in Mombasa, and then had his own engineering business. Until the UK government cuts came, Philip had planned to send his son to a British university. Kishore Jacob, son of Wasant Jacob one of our leading headmasters, obtained an educational appointment in Bahrain. My godson Sherad, son of Manohar Shende our friend and bearer, went on to run a secretarial school in Nagpur and in Chandrapur. And so one could go on.

The beginnings of a Christian School on the veranda of the Govt. Forest Office in Padmapur

We must have taken it for granted that our teachers, men and women, would be in the forefront of their profession. I do not remember a bad report from the government inspectors on any school. Almost as soon as a school was opened, it seemed that we earned a government grant to cover salaries. At one time or another, I suppose every outstation had its primary school, until they were handed over to the government. In Chanda, of course, the boys' and girls' schools were separate, middle as well as primary, each with a staff of four.

In more recent times, popular demand from the city has led to the opening of English language schools, in Chandrapur.

In the time of Archdeacon Yohan and Miss Ward, in 1965, a divinity school was started in Naginabag, for the Marathi speaking Dioceses of Nasik, Bombay, and Nagpur. The school supplied a need for five years, and then sensibly closed when the need ceased.

The hospital, being a women's hospital and open to Hindus and Muslims as well as Christians, men hardly entered. Our job was to keep it provided, and even to buttress a sagging wall, since it was built on "cotton" soil. There were some twenty-two beds, with at times fewer patients and sometimes twice as many. The dispensary, and village work, must have benefited many thousands, in and around Chandrapur.

FIRE FIGHTING

They used to say that the missionary nurses had to be prepared to do what doctors and surgeons do in Britain. The ordinary missionary too has to be a jack of all trades. One morning near Gadicurla some forty miles to the east of Chandrapur, I was after a black buck for the pot, when we noticed a huge column of smoke going up from the village. Clearly it was on fire. Remembering Drake and Nelson, I did my duty by the local Christians and got the buck, then handed the rifle to my helper and raced for the village. Soon we found a path, and ended up at a run. As we went, I warned the man that we might have to force people to tear down their houses, or do anything else that I said. He was to take care of the rifle.

Soon we found ourselves in a crowd in front of a roaring inferno. There was no one in any of the houses. But little was being done. Twenty men were hounded and encouraged to go off and get water. The roofs were just then falling in, and moving round to the leeward, I found some neighbouring roofs unguarded or guarded by only one man. So I set about organising the fire-watching. Seizing on the nearest unfortunates, I hurled them onto the roof. Probably fright kept them there. Most of the owners had a small pot of water up on the roof and nothing else. Searching by the light of the flames in the little byres and stables, I tore out from the walls and mangers small wattle hurdles and flung them up on to the roofs – "If the fire comes with this 'maro' – beat it out for all you are worth." Soon water began to arrive, and volunteers and pressed men on the roofs were persuaded to part for the moment with their small reserve of water and to set about soaking the whole roof. On the more exposed roofs I threw up huge wattle hurdles, as being less inviting to the flames. One man was on a little dog-kennel of a place, within three feet of a flaming house. How his escaped I don't know, unless being a small house he had really soaked the roof. The roof of the next house had fallen in. That danger was past; but the wall might go at any time. It seemed obvious that the little house should be demolished, or at least that the thatch should come off. "Either you take off the thatch or I will myself." And I began to tear it off with an axe. Obviously I was only exposing unsoaked thatch. So I moved on, giving instructions to all and sundry. "If this catches, tear the whole house down."

Soon it seemed that, if the wind were kind, the fire would not spread. But there was still chance enough for the wind. And as it veered a little, new danger spots appeared. I found one roof almost overhanging a furnace of fallen roof and thatch, sheltered only by the still standing walls of the house. That I demanded should be guarded all night, and soaked again and water flung over the still standing wall. Sure enough, when we came next day we saw that the roof had later caught in places. In another place we tried to save some rice, on which a burning roof had fallen. And some of it did appear next day, roasted but eatable. At another place we gathered a band of stalwarts to tear down a burning roof. Then round and round I went raucously exhorting all and sundry to keep on watering the ruins for days. Then home.

Next morning off went a chit to the District Commissioner asking for free timber and grass for the villagers. Perhaps it was on account of that that the rumour got about that I had rebuilt the houses in the night. In fact I hardly dared to go to the burnt village, for fear I should be mobbed by irate housewives who had lost their water pots – possibly all they had saved from the fire. But the only complaint we heard was about a water pot which had not been returned. And even for that I was not blamed; in fact our arrival was said to have hastened the return. All the same, I seemed to recognise it as the one I had thrown to the man with the dog-kennel house. Later I returned my axe to its owner whom we found digging in the ruins of his home.

In the burnt village we sang and preached and sold books. Then moved on to lovely Gowardhan. Lunch and a bath were ready and, if not yet drinking water, at least plenty of tea to drink.

Scottish Churchman, October 1944.

CHANDA TOURING AGAIN

In the morning, a bank draft of Rs. 14,000 had come from Bombay, and news of some of our lost luggage shipped in the Georgic. There were letters to be written about that, and one to the Archdeacon about the condition of cemeteries and the scattered graves of British soldiers. Then, should we admit a girl whose mother had just died to the Hostel? That could safely be left to Mrs. Hall. The Income Tax had to be placated on behalf of the whole staff. A returned Christian prisoner of war wanted to know where his family allotment had gone, and now that he had taken to himself a wife, it hardly satisfied him that his elder sister had kept his brothers and sisters alive and well. A Brahmin from Bellarshar came saying he wanted to be a Christian, whereas it seemed pretty clear he only wanted a recommendation to get work. All the same, someone had to be found to follow him up in his home town: a catechist who was going to relieve a master who was sick: he would see to it. And so we came to lunch, and to set out.

I was paying my first visit to the Christian community at Gadicurla. (While I had been on furlough they had been making history. Never before had there been a Christian of this village or of these parts.) The cycles had gone on by rail, by the little jungle narrow-gauge line. We had the little car, and a road that made driving crazy work. But we reached Mul. I found various subordinates of the police at the Dak Bungalow. I had tea. We inspected the new cook-house at Mul, with the Christian builder who had begged a lift in the car. It seemed good work, but was still unfinished. We sounded local opinion and discussed ways and means of getting to Gadicurla, where I was due to celebrate next morning. In the end I abandoned the cycle and decided to walk.

I went lightly laden, with vessels and vestments and shaving kit and pyjama shorts and mosquito net and prayer book in a small kit bag. A Bible was too heavy, and I knew I would find one at the other end. I had gym shoes as a gesture against various diseases caught in the mud, and an old Bisley hat and waterproof as at least a gesture of protection against the rain.

A River Crossing

We had chosen the shortest route, and at first everyone assured me that I would have to swim the river about 200 yards across. Later there were rumours of a dug-out tree-trunk ferry. I passed dozens of people, bent double in the mud, hidden in their bamboo and leaf waterproofs, transplanting rice. They assured me there were fishermen at the river, but I wondered unkindly if that were just to save the embarrassment of further demands. The track I had not seen before. It almost petered out in a wilderness, when suddenly I found myself on the river bank, away in the distance a little group, and below them the dark outline of the ferry nosing into the bank.

"Will you go soon?" I had expected a weary wait. But they had obviously seen me far off, and had awaited my arrival. "Can you tell me the way to Pisculi?" It was a village halfway on my road. And again my luck was in. I found that my neighbour in the canoe was a leading man of the village. Later he proved to be slow. But he put me on the right track, and I pressed on. I passed a fine black buck with a family of eight.

By now I knew almost every inch of the ground, and it was good to see it again. For six months of the year it is wet. But it was at its wettest now. I recognized the little hill where I had planned a Balhousie Castle in Perth. On its top I had once taken a photo of Waman Ramteke, one of our catechists, and had called it "The promised land."

Gadicurla

I saw the hill of Gadicurla, and then the trees of the village, tamarinds soft and rounded in the dimming light, from olive to darkest green; here and there a red-tiled roof showing through, and all festooned with the blue smoke of the evening meal. I thought of that visit nearly seven years before, when Waman and I had stumbled on the village for the first time. We had paused there for ten minutes, sold out of gospels, and passed on. Some of those gospel readers still have to come in. But now there is the beginning of a Christian community where there was none before, and a house where a catechist can stay not ten minutes, but twelve months of the year.

My heart was very thankful as I covered the last half-mile in the growing darkness. In the jungle, a shepherd had taken one look at me in my cassock and fled. The villagers were more friendly. I swung round a corner and heard voices. There on the gable in front of me was a huge upstanding cross. I had arrived.

I was happy. The house and veranda and little sanctuary seemed as good, in fact, as we had planned. This was the spearhead of the Christian advance. To-morrow I would meet Christians where there had been no Christians before. From the bungalow I could see palm trees silhouetted against the fast-fading light, and the fireflies in the trees seemed to join in my evensong.

Scottish Guardian, 27th September 1946.

Gadicurla

GADICURLA DRY

Last time I wrote of Gadicurla it was sopping. The next time I went it was only wet. This time it was dry. After the usual rush of paying out money, writing recommendations, dealing with Hostel needs, and all the rest that had to be done, my wife and I set off with the dog and the cat and the little car.

It was dark soon after we left Mul on our cycles, and the kitten quickly learned why I had planned to do that bit in day-light. Several times I fell off, with her basket in or out of hand, but only once did a startled face peer out from beneath the lid. (It is surprising how difficult it is to see a rut even in the light of a full moon.) However, at last we left the road and took to the canal path, where there was nothing to fear if one could keep to a strip six inches wide. Finally we got to Gadicurla, and baths, and dinner, and Evensong, and bed.

Next morning there was a Sung Eucharist for the two families. The third, in spite of all our admonitions, was absent as the father was away. But as they are the best of the bunch, we did not mind so much. After the Creed they were catechised on their Confirmation preparation: "God the Father who made me and all the world, God the Son … God the Holy Ghost."

"Do British Children Talk English?"

This time we were out primarily for the sake of the Christian community. We did not have to spend our time going to distant villages. I was taken out on shikar (shooting for food) in the middle of the day, rather protesting. We drew blank. Most of the day was spent visiting Krushna Paulus and his family, and trying to persuade the Mahar neighbours to take a sick woman in to hospital. Again we went out before dusk. Again we drew a blank. I was failing in part of my duty. But our vain attempt at shikar provided me with an extra oppportunity for catechising, and I improved the twilight hour on our way home by drawing out from Hurri Thoma the meaning of his baptism. He answered well. Meanwhile my wife had been receiving a call from some Brahmin girls, bright and friendly, but strangely unsophisticated, asking in Marathi. "In your country do even the little children talk English?"

Next morning the Eucharist sung again. If there were no Christians working temporarily at Mul, it was a 100 per cent attendance for Christians at least twenty miles around. We ran rather hurriedly over one's duty to God and to one's neighbour. Then photographs, mainly for Cpl. Myles of the Black Watch who had helped to draw the plans of the building. (This was the building being measured out, and these were the catechumens, in the Chanda Film.)

Rex Again

Our third and last night, we had asked the whole Christian "mundlie" to dinner. Fowls were unobtainable, or fabulously dear. I was by common consent ordered out again on shikar. No buck were reported, except somewhere vaguely over the horizon. We left about half-past ten, and on our way back, Rex almost blotted his copy-book over some sheep. But order was quickly restored, and we strode on. Suddenly, against all the rules, Hurri pointed excitedly, and there, 500 yards away, were some buck.

There seemed to be no cover, except a lone tree with a six inch trunk. That might have done for a single beast, but not for half a dozen. I fancied there was a small nalla ahead, but probably too near the buck to be of any use. Then I spotted a new rice bund, about three feet high. I made for that, away from the buck, then doubled up and doubled back. As soon as I had the rifle over the top, the buck started to move. But I got onto him again and let fly – a most un-Bisley-like shot from a rest for my hand. He shied away, slowly lolloped a few yards, fell over, and lay.

Black buck

As soon as he was sure the buck was dead, Rex took shelter in a crack in the ground about five feet deep. He scraped away the soil and sat in the damp earth. I took his tip, and joined him, while the others got a pole. The buck was a good weight for two, and as I looked at Hurri, I concluded this was not a fit time for catechising. We had got our dinner, and were back in time for twelve o'clock lunch.

We spent the early evening visiting, watching all the processes of weaving, and, it seemed, successfully persuading the sick woman's relations to take her in to hospital.

The dinner that night was impressive – people who less than a year ago were outcastes, sitting eating with us in the moonlight in the face of all the world. More impressive still were the family prayers that followed. Those same people joined in all the responses, said the Creed and the Gloria. When it came to praying silently for the sick woman, one felt that the whole congregation was really at prayer.

As we parted they thanked us as charmingly as any could. And why not? They are no longer outcastes. As they told me only yesterday, they are "Members of Christ ... and inheritors of the Kingdom of Heaven."

Scottish Guardian, 29th November 1946.

BISHOP HANNAY'S TOUR

In 1947 Bishop Hannay of Argyll was Convener of the Overseas Mission Board in Scotland. That winter, he made a tour of St John's Diocese in Kaffraria – a diocese which the Episcopal Church had long helped with money and workers. Then he came on to the Scottish Church's Mission in India, arriving in Bombay on 16th December.

Quotations are from his report in the **Scottish Guardian,** February and March 1948.

In Bombay the Bishop was met by the Superior of the Cowley Fathers. "I got through the Customs with no trouble. I had expected that the exercise of a new authority (after Independence) might make for fussiness." "The kindness and courtesy I received was what one expects from the Society of St. John the Evangelist as a marked characteristic."

The Bishop came by night from Bombay. "The carriage was so badly lighted that reading was impossible; I slept but little; and in consequence passed nearly thirteen hours of darkness in sheer boredom." He travelled with a Muslim, who made his devotions publicly. "I wondered what he thought of me, as I was plainly a Christian clergyman, who apparently did not do much about his religion; but I did not explain that I had said my office long before he was awake."

"We reached Chanda at long last at one o'clock, only twenty minutes late." There the Bishop received a great welcome, with garlands galore. "A lot of local notabilities (Indian) were asked to tea to meet me, which was rather a strain when there was little common ground on which to build a conversation." However the Bishop found that the Indian District Commissioner was a fellow Cambridge man. "He spoke highly of the Mission Staff, and said he was sure that under the new regime Christians would get a square deal, but without privileges. I replied that I cared nothing about the privileges of an establishment: Christianity must and could stand on its own feet." (This DC must, I think, have been Mr Atal, who later became the Indian Ambassador in Washington. He met my elder daughter and her husband in London many years later, and gave them a most kindly welcome in Jaipur when they visited India.)

The next day the Bishop was introduced to the Mothers' Union by Mrs Molly Hall. The day following meant an early start, to a village where Cuthbert Hall had spent the night. Mr Hall celebrated, and then made four people catechumen. "So the Church grows, and not least surely when it grows slowly." In the girls' school "Each class sang to me; but they cannot sing like the Bantu in Kaffraria; their voices are naturally harsh." We felt the same about the Bishop and his judgements on India! Bishop Hannay had been a missionary in South Africa.

Then the Bishop was going to Nagpur to meet Bishop Hardy and for the ordination of the Revd Paul Yohan. The Grand Trunk Express was due at 5.15 a.m., but on enquiry it was said to be four hours late, so the Bishop returned to bed. Of course we were sleeping in the open. Two hours later, we heard the train in the distance. So, without outward haste, I invited the Bishop to go to the station as the train would soon come in. As soon as the Bishop was gone, I called to the Revd John Towers, and asked him to cycle to the station and hold up the train till the Bishop was on board. He had good reason to think he had done the job, chatting to the driver for ten minutes. To our astonishment, when the car got back, the Bishop got out and walked silently to his room. Our driver explained that when the Bishop got to the station he went into the empty booking hall, and kept demanding a ticket: "I want a ticket to Nagpur." Meanwhile, our anxious driver with a mixture of Marathi and physical force tried to get the Bishop to board the train. But the Bishop was a stickler for propriety, and stuck to the platform.

What to do? There was no other train. Petrol was still rationed and we had none. I cycled to the station, and found a goods train getting up steam.

"Would you take a Bishop to Nagpur?"

"Delighted. But we won't get there until nightfall."

I doubted if the Bishop would survive that. Then the stationmaster had a brainwave. A very spruce shopkeeper-trader had just arrived, wanting to get to Nagpur. Turning to him, the stationmaster said, "You can easily find petrol. The sahib has a car. Why not pool your resources and join forces." The agreement was made. When he left, about ten o'clock, we told the Bishop we had given him peacock sandwiches, and were rewarded with the first smile of the day.

That was not the end of trouble for David our driver. In our relief, we had forgotten to bargain for petrol for the return journey. David had to spend an extra day in Nagpur, hunting for petrol. Nor was that the end of travel trouble for the Bishop. Coming back, he was accompanied by the Revd J K Towers and Mrs Towers. They got to

Wardha, Mr Ghandi's town, half-way home, without mishap. They were to wait some hours for the Grand Trunk going south to Chanda. As the time drew near, they were told the Express would be late ... then later ... then very late. Nobly, the Towers shared their meagre bedding, and found the Bishop some food. Even the slow train was late next day. Perhaps they came on the Grand Trunk after all.

The poor Bishop had more to suffer. We had got the impression that India compared poorly with Africa, where it seemed catechumens were raked in like autumn leaves. In Nasik diocese numbers were greater than with us. We had known Archdeacon Batty at language school, we were with him on the train when it was announced "Belgium has fallen", and he had taken village retreats in Chanda. The Battys kindly agreed to entertain the Bishop and to show him round.

All went well on the train until the Bishop found himself in a siding. A train drew in: "Where is this going?"

"To Ahmadnagar, Sahib."

"Why, that's just what I want." and in he got. In the middle of the night, another siding: "Why are we stopped?"

"We have to wait, Sahib, for the Ahmadnagar express to pass."

So the Bishop got in seven hours late; the Archdeacon got a pass to break the curfew, and still greeted the Bishop with a smile.

The Bishop's own account in the **Scottish Guardian** was only a little different: "The next day was spent in alternate spasms of fury and boredom, thanks to the lunatic advice of a stationmaster. One naturally pays attention to stationmasters and their words, but in this case the result was to miss a connection at Manmad, and eight hours of nothing to do until 9 p.m. Cynically I felt the place was well named." (In his vexation, the Bishop was mentally mispronouncing Munmaad.)

We were full of admiration for the way Bishop Hannay plodded round the country alongside a bullock cart at two and a half miles an hour. And he seemed to enjoy the Christmas camp at Junona, though the life must have been strange to him and it had some trying moments. It was there that Mrs Copland heard of the death of her father, who, as it happened, was born in a CMS Mission in our Diocese. And it was at Junona that the babes were nearly lost in the wood. More of that later.

Bishop Hannay at Ahiri

In his report, Bishop Hannay complained that the Mission complex had no chapel. That was accurate, except for the girls' hostel chapel holding fifty to sixty, and the chapel in the ladies' bungalow seating ten to twelve. The Revd Dr K W Mackenzie, then rector in Monifieth, was not impressed. **Scottish Guardian,** July 1948: "The convener of the Overseas Mission Board in his recently published report on his visit to Chanda and Kaffraria begins his report on Chanda with the words 'The district for which we are supposed to be responsible is the Civil District of Chanda, which is impossible.' And he adds later 'We have so far only touched one small corner.' The statement has a defeatist ring about it, and, with all due respect to the Bishop, one cannot but feel that he has brought back a very erroneous impression of the nature and extent of the work in Chanda; and it is fortunate that our Missionaries in the field have not only attempted the impossible, but have had considerable success in covering the area."

CHRISTMAS CAMP

The day after Christmas, the boys' and the girls' hostels, I suppose to the number of sixty or seventy children, and all the missionary families, went into camp on the edge of a huge old Gond irrigation tank at Junona, some seven miles into the jungle from Chanda. It certainly was quite an undertaking, setting it up and provisioning it, but Ruben Master the mission clerk saw to it that all went smoothly.

We lived in tents, old and not so old, preserved and not so well preserved from the white ants through the rest of the year. Some were in regular use for evangelistic touring. The boys made leaf shelters for themselves. The swimming was wonderful, just not too hot. Dr Mackenzie had provided a small canvas boat, and the Glasgow Layman's Movement after the war sent us a tiny rubber dinghy with a sail. These gave much enjoyment. For swimming of course the sexes were carefully segregated. We could stay in the water for any length of time, and there was good diving from the masonry at the side of the tank. Some sort of shikar was expected, and that entailed going off in a rough, jolting bullock cart, shivering, at the crack of dawn. Sometimes we saw tiger pug marks as big as plates, but never a tiger. Each day began with an open air Eucharist, everyone muffled up in sweaters and scarves. In the evening, after prayers, we all sat round a glorious log fire. It was then that the mimics and comics among the boys came into their own. I remember Cuthbert Hall and I rather cheated, shooting at tennis balls flung up in the air. That must have been our first winter, before the war, when cartridges were cheap. It was all too easy, a sitting shot, if

Junona Christmas Camp: Daily Eucharist

you took the ball at the top of its trajectory.

At Junona we once shot a python. Some may today think that a pity, but it was said to have eaten a kid, and there was the usual tale of a child having gone missing.

Twice Padre Leslie Pennell, later Provost of Inverness Cathedral, joined us in Christmas Camp. I don't know what his rank was then, but I think he ended up as Assistant Chaplain General. One morning he was invited to celebrate, in English. Half-way through the service, he fainted. So in proper style we dragged the body aside, another priest got a stole, and carried on. His own description in a letter to a friend (the Revd N Pollock) is only slightly different. "As I knelt for the Prayer of Humble Access, I toppled over in a faint. I came round to find them putting blankets round me, and a pillow under my head. Charles said he would finish the service, and gave me communion, just as I lay beside the altar. It would sound incredible in a church, but was all so fitting and natural out there in God's great Cathedral of Nature. My temperature was 105 degrees, but after two days it was down to 102, and I was taken back to the Mission. Later, Bishop Hardy arrived to stay for four days – a real spiritual giant with a most lovely face and the added charm and attraction of a faint Irish brogue. On Sunday the sung Eucharist at 8 a.m. was to an Indian setting written by one of the Wantage Sisters from Poona. The Bishop preached in Hindi. In the evening at the little English Church (English spoken) he preached one of the greatest sermons I have ever heard on the spiritual lessons to be learnt from the war. Two days later I set off to return to the noise, bustle and clamour of guns, tanks and aeroplanes."

That was the second visit Leslie Pennell had paid to us. Of the first, he had written to the same friend: "The journey involved a round trip of 2,300 miles and I reached Chanda at 2 a.m. It was a great joy at that cold and unfriendly hour to be welcomed in the dark station by a figure in white cassock with a lantern in his hand … I said farewell thanking God afresh for the vision, foresight, and great work accomplished by Bishop Wood, and now so ably carried on by the present regime … I thought of that figure with the lamp, representing the work of our Mission – causing the light of the Gospel to shine in the dark."

BABES IN THE WOOD

In October 1947 the Revd J K Towers came, from Coatbridge, Peebles, and Dundee Cathedral. Soon afterwards in December, Miss Helen Wells arrived to join her brother in the work of the Mission.

When he was coming out, the Scottish Bishops had made it clear that they didn't expect John Towers to get married during his first term of service. Fair enough. No promise had been given. It was soon clear that they were in for a surprise.

Naturally, it was not easy for Europeans to conform to our Indian conventions for engaged couples but on this occasion they were well and truly chaperoned. At the Junona Christmas Camp, Helen and John had very kindly taken a dozen or so of the smallest hostel boys and girls for a walk round the tank after tea.

When dusk fell, they were not back. Very properly, we decided to carry on with evening prayers. Then we set out to look for them – George Wells and I, in different sorts of loco parentis, with others from the camp, a petromax lamp, and a shot gun. We met some of the villagers going out to guard their crops, and with risky kindness they offered to join us. Soon we picked out Miss Wells' shoe marks, and followed them for some way on a sandy jungle track. The track left the waterside and got more and more stony and overgrown. We lost all trace of them. In the end, I was glad that it was George Wells who suggested there was no point in going on: we should have to give up. Then one of the villagers exclaimed "Sahib, shoot off your gun!" I let off a shot, some leaves quietly floated down, and then from far, far away, we heard a shout. On we went, shouting and listening, shouting and listening. The shouts began to come away off the track to the side. We did not want to get lost in turn, and we had no crumbs to mark our way, so every twenty yards or so, we left someone, so that we could find our way back to the track. We found the party, rather disconsolate and frightened, prepared to be cold and hungry. Soon we were on the road home, back at the camp, and fed.

Amusingly, they had followed almost exactly the steps of Miss Smyth and some hostel children at what may have been the first Junona

Christmas Camp in 1903. But Miss Smyth recorded that they "kept in sight of the lake all the way."

Ordinarily on shikar, or going from village to village, I never went into the jungle on my own. The villagers knew every stick and stone. But at Axapur my wife and I nearly got lost. We had only gone out for a stroll at dusk, and suddenly we found it was dark and we did not know the way back. There was no use wandering and little use in sitting under a tree, though we knew they would come searching in time from the Forest Bungalow. Then we heard the bells of a ringi, a trotting cart. It was going fast, but we managed to follow its direction to the main road and so to the bungalow.

In my early days, I was the proud possessor of a four-inch-to-the-mile map, only I had not noted that it was made in 1883. I was staying in a huge thatched forest bungalow, while Canon Patwardhan put up in a Gond village. I joined the Canon early for the Eucharist, and those were the days of fasting communion. Then I was to cycle back only three or four miles, for breakfast at the bungalow. The map showed a direct route, but the Canon pointed out another way: "I think, Sir, this way would be better. But do whichever you like." I liked the shortness and certainty of the map. After a mile, the road faded out. I could go back. But I was going in the right direction, heading south for the main road. I had only to carry on to meet it. And there was a fire line – a wide swaith cleared of trees – ahead. To be effective, the fire line would go on till it met the road. I took it, pushing the cycle. The fire line became indistinct, and I was pushing the bike over boulders and through long grass above my head. It was hard going. Then there was just jungle. I met a wild bison, a gaur, face to face. We looked at each other, and passed on our different ways. The bicycle came in two, and it was not that sort. The road could not be far off. I struggled on with the bicycle bits under my arm. In the end, I did come to the road and the bungalow, about 3 p.m. I was so thirsty that I could not eat for some time. But I had learnt my lesson early – to trust the local people! And the Chanda blacksmith mended my cycle, I suspect for the second time.

As a matter of interest, the government one-inch maps covered the whole district, and were most accurate, even showing furlong stones on the main roads. The simplest villager could give directions: "Go along to the third furlong, and then turn right across the fields."

With decimalization I hope the maps are still as good.

EPISCOPAL PRESSURES

During the meetings of the Representatives Church Council in Edinburgh in 1950, Bishop Hannay (Convener of the Overseas Board) asked me to see him. He said that Bishop Sinker had written to say he thought it best that I should not return to Chanda. Hannay suggested I cable my resignation. (Only recently I have seen a letter in the CWMA archives, which shows Bishop Sinker writing that the other missionaries had agreed with him that Copland should not return. Today, those missionaries have no recollection of expressing such a sentiment. Was Bishop Sinker being "economical of the truth", or had he honestly misinterpreted some remark to support his policy?)

Soon after Bishop Hannay had spoken to me, Bishop Warner of Edinburgh and Provost Gooderham from the Cathedral got in touch with me. After some discussion they suggested that I do nothing. That is exactly what I did.

Having noted that little incident, it is perhaps not out of place to quote from the **Scottish Churchman** of May 1951 a report of my return, by the Revd G R Wells, who had been in charge during my furlough: "The platform was crowded with people – some of them travellers, but the majority friends who had come to meet our returning traveller; there were young men, who had managed to get an hour's leave from work; masters and teachers from our own and from the local High Schools; all the Mission Padres – Canon Patwardhan from Durgapur, the Revd. B.Y. Salve, and the Revd. H. Jagtap from Bhandak; catechists and Mission servants; some Government officials; Christians and non-Christians; and everywhere children of all sizes, all beaming and many clutching little leaf packets containing garlands. There was an amazing diversity in the members of the crowd, and the presence of some was surprising, because one had not realized before that they had any interest in our little world. Truly, Mr. Copland's friends are many and various! I was asked very severely by one of them why I had not given the school a holiday on such a day.

The bell rang, and the train came rumbling into the station. At the open door of one compartment stood a white-clad figure, and as soon as it was seen there rose a shout of joy from the children and youths, and the whole crowd began to run along with the train. It was an amazing demonstration of affection – very moving in its spontaneity."

When I got home from that furlough in February 1951, I found the Mission stocked up with "unfermented grape juice" for the Holy Communion.

Previously I had heard Bishop Sinker state in conversation that at the Passover all yeast was thrown out, so there could have been no wine available at the Last Supper. After Bishop Hardy had retired, I regarded Bishop Noel Hall of Chota Nagpur as my ecclesiastical mentor. He had been a great friend of Bishop Wood, and was himself a product of the excellent Dublin University Mission. When I consulted him, he laughed the idea out of court: no one had put any yeast into the wine. Later, he said that if the worst came to the worst and no wine was available, the next best thing would be to squeeze the juice out of some grapes: that would at least be pure, and it would be in the way to becoming wine. Whereas 'unfermented grape juice' must have been adulterated to keep it from fermenting. On no account should we use that.

I found that Bishop Sinker had issued an order that 'unfermented grape juice' be used, "Since wine is not available". The priests in the Mission had no experience of bishops going astray, and had swallowed it all. So began a lengthy saga. Unless he genuinely misunderstood about the Passover yeast, I think the Bishop must have given his order in an attempt to remove a possible stumbling block to reunion with Protestant brethren.

I trod delicately, and was careful to deal only with the local situation. Chanda and, I suppose, most of the Diocese, was a 'dry' area. I wrote that in Chanda we could obtain a licence to import Communion wine from Bombay: would he please withdraw his order insofar as it concerned the Chanda Mission. He would not. I got a licence and imported wine from Bomaby, as previously. And I gained golden opinions by presenting four dozen bottles of the 'unfermented grape juice' to our neighbouring American Mission a hundred miles to the south.

Our Diocesan clerical retreats were great events. They were taken by such men as Bishop Azariah of Dornikal – the first Indian Anglican Bishop – Bishop Christopher Robinson of Lahore, or by one of the Cowley Fathers. Once the Revd. R. C. Hastie Smith was able to join us, when he was an army chaplain. We lived luxuriously, in huge tents, though I remember one of them made an impressive sight when it went up in flames.

With the question of the wine still unsolved, I went to Nagpur for a retreat. Before it began, I visited the chief Enforcement Office, and asked for a permit to buy a bottle of Communion Wine. "Why bother? Your Bishop already has a licence."

"He assures me he has not."

"But most certainly he has a licence."

"Never mind: may I have a permit for one bottle."

With the licence in my pocket, I went and bought the bottle, and had it with me throughout the retreat. On the Sunday morning before the Eucharist in the Cathedral, I met the Bishop and told him I was going to give a bottle of wine at the Offertory. "How did you get it?"

"I got a licence when we came to Nagpur; and they said you already had a licence."

On return to Chanda, I wrote again humbly asking the Bishop to cancel his order with regardto Chanda, since we could import wine from Bombay. Nothing happened. We were perhaps fortunate, since one of our colliery managers had a brother who was the Metropolitan's Chaplain. Discreet enquiry showed that we could take the matter further. I think it was on 1st April that I wrote to the Metropolitan, asking him to suggest to our Bishop that he rescind his order about the use of 'unfermented grape juice', since wine was obtainable on licence. Some time later, our Bishop wrote round the Diocese saying that the Metropolitan had ordered him to withdraw his direction about unfermented grape juice, since the wine was obtainable on licence. That was quite something, from the first Indian Metropolitan to an English brother.

Dornakal Cathedral

THE METROPOLITAN'S VISIT

Not since the laying of the foundation stone of St Andrews Church in 1902 had a visit from the Metropolitan been recorded.

Somehow we had got the feeling that Bishop Sinker was not altogether pleased with the Scottish Mission. He told us that he had arranged for the Metropolitan to come and visit us. We sensed that it might be Balaam come to curse the outcast Israelites. Bishop Mukerjee had been the head of the Cambridge Mission to Delhi, and then assistant Bishop of Lahore, but he had only been Metropolitan since 1950. My wife and now two children had only recently got home to Chanda, and it was with fear and trembling that we invited the Metropolitan to stay with us. Bishop Sinker was to stay at the other bungalow.

In Chanda: Mary Bai, and Frances born in Ootacamund, 1947, Baptised in Chanda.

The Metropolitan came from 29th November till 1st December 1951. Looking back (**Scottish Churchman,** February 1952) it is astounding how much he was able to fit in. We arranged that he should take part in a first baptism at Ghorpeth, but at the last minute, our Bishop said the baptism should be done at another time. So we went ahead. Ghorpeth had first heard of Christ the Saviour of the world from Canon Philip and his companions in 1903.

At 10 a.m. the Mission car drew up in a cloud of dust at the roadside tank of Ghorpeth. Five minutes later a party arrived over the fields from Saiwan, with the cross at their head. In the tank three Saiwan families were baptized, and one from Ghorpeth.

A 50 m.p.h. rush – no doubt equal to 100 m.p.h. on British roads – took the Head of the Mission to Bhandak in time to greet the Metropolitan and our own Bishop. The Mandli – the Christian community – was blessed, and we moved back to Ghorpeth. The Metropolitan blessed the Christians from the two villages and a six foot cross recently presented by Captain and Mrs Phillipps of Edinburgh. So to Sakherwai, though only the brave mission Austin Seven could make the cross-country journey. The Metropolitan was met with drums and cymbals, and led to the new church where he spoke to the people and blessed them.

That night, the Metropolitan preached at the festal evensong in St Andrew's Church, and next day, St Andrew's Day, he pronounced the absolution and gave the blessing at the sung eucharist. Then he laid the foundation stone of a new parsonage, to be built in memory of Bishop Wood. Later in the morning he had interviews with all the clergy and with some of the lay workers. The clergy and Bajerao, the senior catechist, met him for lunch. In the afternoon, at the desire of the Bishop of Nagpur, we had an extraordinary meeting of the Mission Managing Committee. In the evening the District Commissioner and other leading Indian officials and personalities of Chanda City and their ladies came to do honour to the Metropolitan. And the party over, the girls of the hostel gave him a charming little entertainment. Chatting under the stars after dinner, to us the Metropolitan seemed surprisingly open and confiding.

Next morning, the Metropolitan took part in the sung Eucharist at Durgapur. On the road back to Nagpur he was garlanded by the faithful and catechumens at Chichpalli, and most hospitably entertained by the Towers family at Mul. Sadly, the Towers had received a wire from our Bishop saying they had not time to go a few extra miles to Vihad to meet the people from Saoli, Kapsi, and Gadicurla, who were all converging on Vihad.

The Metropolitan's visit had proved a real encouragement to the staff of the Mission, and to the whole Christian community. It was, I suppose, the first time there had been an Indian Bishop in Chanda. It seemed that Balaam had come to curse and had stayed to bless.

A week or two later the Head of the Mission was honoured by an invitation to be one of the two or three clerical assessors to the Episcopal Synod. In that I think he followed in the footsteps of the Revd Dr K W Mackenzie.

DOST THOU RENOUNCE ...?

What heart-searchings had gone to their decision! Their fields would be taken away from them, people said, and well they knew that such injustice could be done. In the off season, the big landlord would give them no more work – that useful extra which provided ready money for a sari at Divali or for some other big purchase at the Tadali bazaar. More certain than that, "Your jatwallas, caste-fellows will turn against you, and there will be no well in all the village from which you will be allowed to draw water." (Having uttered that warning, there was no need to remind them that the village tank, dirty at the best of times, was empty in the hot weather.) Worse still, "You will find no husbands for your daughters when they grow up, and all the world knows what that will mean." More subtle still, the Devil and some of his friends merely whispered, "It is hard enough to-day, but just you wait till the British Raj is gone, and then you will learn what we do to Christians." Most touchingly their old mother pleaded, "My children, wait: wait until I am gone. You will send my soul to hell, if none of you are here to burn me by the rites of the old religion."

They had nothing to gain, except salvation. And they had literally everything to lose, including the hope of salvation their people had clung to in Hinduism for countless generations. And yet they came. In December 1945 in the face of all the world these four families of Sakerwai publicly accepted Christ as their Saviour, renounced Hinduism, and promised to learn the Christian way of worship and life.

Christmas at Sakherwai

They kept their promise. In February 1947 Padre Jagtap asked me to get the Bishop's leave for their baptism. That was given. Then to fix a date. During Lent we were all weekly treading the outstation roads, all widely scattered. Everything pointed to Holy Saturday, the day before Easter, as being the proper day and if not convenient at least less generally inconvenient than any other.

The catechists, two tents, and my luggage were to go out on Maundy Thursday while we were still at Warora. On Good Friday the Halls came back from Holy Week in Gadicurla. On Saturday morning a servant went ahead by train. At 3.30 the Halls and I set off, at about the hottest part of the day. After eight miles to Tadali, we had to abandon the car. Padre Jagtap, returning to Bhandak from Bellarshah, was just disappearing over the horizon in the direction of Sakerwai. There was a bullock cart for the Halls while I made off on my bicycle which had been left at the station. As I went I remembered a visit with Padre Jagtap before ever Jogi was a catechumen, then camping for a fortnight with them during the catechumenate, then rushing out after a Eucharist in Chanda (in our motorless days) for Jogi's baptism. Later I had baptised others myself. And now here those people were representing the Church Catholic as witnesses and godparents at the baptism of their fellows. The road seemed shorter now. I knew I would find friends.

All were ready, we were told, except one family from an outlying village. The tank was almost empty, so the baptism would have to be alongside the village well. We went along to see that everyone knew what to do and where to do it, that all should be done decently and in order. My Mussalman servant was to take a cine picture from afar.

We returned and waited. We sent word that we would go ahead with those who were present. But the women had turned shy; they would not be baptised without their elder sister from the other village. The husbands were ready, but the women would wait. We refused to baptise bits of a family. But we sent a message to say that any time that evening we were ready to baptise any complete family of the four that came forward. We unrobed and waited, and called the camera home.

Soon Jogi's signal came to us across the tank. We were to come. Hastily we robed again. It seemed one family had the courage to be baptised alone – rather a big thing for them to do. We sent forward all our lanterns. Then we followed in procession round the half-crescent of the high bund of the tank, a catechist carrying the cross on high, Padre Jagtap and Padre Hall, followed by the head of the mission, resplendent in an erstwhile cope of St. Mary's Cathedral in Edinburgh.

As we drew near the well, the Christians burst into song, a Marathi tune known to the youngest in the village, and the words Khrista mazha Taranara – "Christ my Saviour".

On the top of the bank the cross stopped, silhouetted for all the world to see against the evening light. Below was the low parapet of the well, the Padres near, catechumens and Christians grouped in a semi-circle close by, around and beyond, an ever-increasing crowd of villagers. It was the time for drawing water. There was an occasional clank as some woman let down her bucket and rope and gently set down her water pot. But all who came stayed to hear and see.

Each family was being sponsored by one of the Christian families of Sakerwai, and this family had fallen to Kondu. Padre Jagtap took the longer parts of the service, Padre Hall put the questions. Bravely and joyously they answered, and the solemn service went on. "Prabhudas Jaiwant, I baptise thee. ... We receive this person ..." When it came to answering for the children, there was Kondu, tall, dignified, weathered, a true countryman. Determinedly and happily he answered, echoed by cheery, round-faced Bukubai, his wife. "Go ye therefore and teach all nations, baptising them ..." How often one had pondered these words, and here was a response. Our own Scottish Church must have pondered them when, more than half a century ago, she undertook sole responsibility for the fulfilment of that command in this District of Chanda. That day at Sakerwai, we who were from Scotland rejoiced that she had gone one more step forward on the road that she had chosen.

There followed another hymn, and the Blessing. Then we dispersed, Padre Jagtap in a cart through the night to Bhandak, the Halls to Chanda and Bellarshah, Anand and Stephen to Chanda.

It was a strange, hot night of dust and wind. I was greeted in the morning with the news that the outlying family had arrived. Then began the joyous Easter Eucharist. It has been a tremendous privilege to watch the development of this small community from heathendom and then from first beginnings within the Church until to-day. It may not go easily into words, but there is no question that the love and reverence of this Sakerwai congregation is very genuine. For the last time this family of catechumens had to leave after the sermon, and they went out rather sadly. Then joyously they came forward for their baptism. It was something very real to receive them, out there in the open, into the family of Christ's Church.

Scottish Guardian, 9th May 1947.

FIRST COMMUNIONS AGAIN

This time it was Gadicurla. In the morning we had been at Bhandak, sixteen miles north of Chanda, for a celebration. At 5.30 I had to take a mid-week service in Chanda. The idea was to do at least ten miles before dark. But, in fact, it was dusk when we set off. The lights, however, lasted, and we had an uneventful run to Mul. An inspector of schools who came in later reported meeting a fine panther on the road.

Next morning all the Mul congregation turned up. With David the driver it was a 133% attendance; almost enough, I should imagine, to upset the statisticians of the Annual Report in Edinburgh. Even so, we did not manage to sing the whole of the service. We were off by nine o'clock, doing the first four miles in luxury with our bicycles in the car. We reached Gadicurla about 10.30. By then it was really hot, and we almost felt we had already done a day's work. The catechist there drinks boiled water (out of a rather questionable village pond), so I was able to drink and drink and drink, to the amusement of the children and probably to the disorganisation of the household arrangements.

I raised again the question of Pompurna. Pompurna is a big village between Kothari on the southerly Ahiri road, and Gadicurla which lies to the east of Chanda. It is within striking distance from Gadicurla, and I had not been there for a long time. The road is partly jungle, and the catechist pleaded for a return by day-light. That meant starting about one o'clock, and going through the heat of the day. The Andhari river, which once occasioned the loss of a Mission car and some exciting rescues, was now a waste of sand and a mere trickle of water. (I had to run the last fifty yards to a damp patch, as my feet could stand no more.) Beyond the river Bajerao Master found a most welcome school friend, a Mussalman, who filled us up with tea.

We reached Pompurna about three o'clock, and spent most of our time with the Mahars and the Perdhans. As we talked, Kondu joined us. He was my first acquaintance in Pompurna. A gentle man, a weaver, quiet spoken, he had first come up to me in all the dust and turmoil of the weekly bazaar and said, "In your religion, can you meet God?"

Soon he took his leave and said he would see us again at the river, where he had laid out a vegetable garden in the river bed – a brave gamble with the weather even in our climate.

There we later met him and his friend the blind sadu, and went home laden with turbuzes dangling from our handlebars. It was dark, as dark as it can be with a full moon, when we reached the canal seven miles from home. Poor Bajerao suffered from his rectitude. His cycle at one point chose to plunge down the broad slope to the Stygian waters of the canal, and because he himself refused to leave the straight and narrow path, he fell headlong.

At the canal we met the wind. Ordinarily it would have been termed hot. But it was cool and refreshing by comparison with what we had known. Suddenly it brought us great wafts as of a gigantic jam-making. And that was almost exactly what it was – the juice of the sugar cane being boiled in great six-foot pans. Then came the welcome smell of village cooking, and we rounded the hill to find Bajerao's family coming out to welcome us.

It was after eight o'clock when we got back. First communions next day, so after filling up with water, we went to visit the two Christian homes for prayers. Krushna Paulus had fever, so we had to persuade a brother to brave the terrors of the tank path to come and get some quinine. Shanti, Hurri's wife, was reported to have turned over a new leaf, and I suggested that Bajerao prayed that she would soon be ready for confirmation and able to make her first communion. Instead, Bajerao began by giving thanks that Shanti was living at peace with her husband, and so went on to pray for her preparation. It was, of course, a very proper subject for thanks in that house. But I wondered how many of us in Britain would have taken it as properly as Shanti did. We parted with smiles all round. Thereafter confessions. It was ten by the time I had a much needed bath, and some time after eleven when I got to bed.

We were up before six to a glorious fresh morning. It must have been about 7.15 when Bajerao reported the Church in Gadicurla all present and correct. It was a joyous service for us all – Krushna Paulus very solemn, his wife with her baby happy and at home in this new-found holiness, little Hurri Thoma obviously happy and yet solemnly determined at the same time, Shanti, as usual, rather taken up with her baby, but she and Chandrasheker, Paulus' ten-year-old boy, looking forward to their own confirmation and communions. Such is the beginning of the Church holy catholic and apostolic in those parts. There were also six of Bajerao Master's family, and my servant Manohar.

Afterwards Manohar gave us tea, sweetened for those who liked it with the local sugar, the gul we had smelt boiling. We had some amusement over the photographs I had taken last time. It was decided Manohar was to return to Mul to search for wheat (now off the market). I set off for Chamursi about ten o'clock. But that story has been told before – the dust and the steady grind, the Waingunga where one felt it was too much trouble to bathe, the red, rutted road driving ever on over a country now harvested and become rather desolate, the ever-increasing heat. Then a drink from the duffedar's family, and this written in the coolness of the cells or whatever they call the part of the police station I am allowed to occupy. Tomorrow is Saturday, and I must be back in Chanda for a Mothers' Union service at five o'clock.

Scottish Guardian, 11th July 1947.

FAR TRAVEL

Missionaries stationed in the foot hills always went to the same hill station. We were pledged to go to the hills for a month in the hot weather and I suppose we shared it out between, say the 10th April and the 15th June. In Chandrapur we were lucky being right in the middle of India: we could go south to Ootacamund, where my wife's cousin was Collector and where Frances was born, or to Simla where the Studdert Kennedys (formerly DUM) befriended me in the rectory and whence I cycled over the Jalori Pass to the Kulu Valley, with Chandu Ray, soon to be ordained, and later a bishop; or to Darjeeling to see an old Cambridge friend, George Wells, and to go to Sikkim, leaving splodges of red on the dak bungalow carpet or elsewhere, as a result of leeches.

In Simla I met some men of the Lancashire Fusiliers, who had just got out of Burma. They were very hard hit in spirit. But the Karens, anti-aircraft gunners I think, who got out with them, had plenty of spunk left.

One hot weather I went to Landour, I think it was, with Bob Sawyer, a Cuddesdon friend from the Oxford Mission in Calcutta. We felt so lazy that we started to learn Urdu: aik shuherse aurut pani burrene aie. Later, somewhere in the north, perhaps going to Darjeeling, I found myself travelling with men of the Black Watch. They had been at Allemain, and told me of a Forfar friend, David Greenhill-Gardyne, who was killed there.

With the hot weather coming, I did not mind watching the thermometer climbing to 110 degrees. After that, as it climbed to 115 or more, I thought it bad for one's mental health to watch it! It was rather similar to catching mosquitos in mid-air. When successful, the effort was rewarding. When one began to miss, I thought it was time to stop. Chandrapur was not particularly exceptional in its heat. It was rather more distinguished in never getting cold.

When first we went to India in 1938, of course by train we travelled first-class. Those were the days when even tourist passengers, like missionaries, on board ship donned a dinner jacket in the evenings.

Next, it was second class. I doubt if we ever got to Inter. Then it was third. I have travelled third from Madras to Darjeeling and to Simla, but never, I am glad to say, at one fell swoop. Probably we did not tell the Board in Edinburgh: they might have been shocked. In Madras I got to the station early, and found luxury: there were two luggage racks, one on top of the other. The top rack, about a foot from the roof, afforded me very comfortable sleeping quarters. In khaki, one might have felt a bit ashamed at being a "poor European". In a white cassock, one was always assured of a friendly and honoured welcome.

At least when we first went to India, it was customary for visitors to bring their bearers and their own bedding – sheets, pillow and mosquito net. The custom made for the building of friendship among the servants as well as the masters. And no doubt the custom made it easier for people to descend unexpectedly on another family. There was a tale of Miss Molly Mackenzie, waking in the middle of the night, to see a figure in breeches lying on another bed on the veranda. She was on the point of summoning somebody; it would not have been the police. (It was said that the DC had a telephone, but no one else had one in Chanda.) Then she saw that the figure was a lady missionary friend from the neighbouring American Mission at Sironcha, 120 miles to the south. All was well.

Nowadays, third class travel is probably much grander. Towards the end of our time, they introduced a Janta Express from Madras to Delhi, going through Chandrapur. It was third class, but much less crowded than the ordinary train. One hot weather we started in the Janta Express going to Kashmir. Jane, a baby of eleven months, got bitten by something and her lip swelled up like a balloon. Frances, just over four, came out in blotches with a fever and my wife thought it looked like bubonic plague. When after the thirty-six hour journey we arrived in Delhi, we were staying with the Boses. Mr Vivian Bose was a Supreme Court Judge and his wife was a daughter of the famous missionary of 1910 vintage, John Mott. As it happened, Mrs Bose had accepted a challenge to produce an old-fashioned sixteen course dinner for a dozen people. Every second course or so, my wife was called away to deal with the ayah and her two patients. Next day, the children went to St Stephen's Hospital of the SPG, and Jane bears the mark of their healing knife to this day. Frances' cure was completed by a Russian doctor in Shrinagar. We were most grateful, but we wondered: traditionally, India has always been suspicious of Russians on the northern border. St Stephen's kept its centenary with much public thanksgiving, in 1985.

Towards the end of the war, the government or the Chaplain General or someone very kindly allowed us to go to the UK on leave by troopship. Cuthbert Hall went first and I followed a year later. For me, VE day came on the Red Sea or the Suez Canal, and there was almost a riot. The officers were given two bottles of beer, the men only one. It was amusing when we got to very much bombed Liverpool: the men I had travelled with all had first-class passes and had to sit up four a side, while I had a third compartment to myself. It was as good as Madras.

Axapur P.W.D. bungalow

TOURING

Touring made up so much of our lives, that I am sure it should have a heading of its own. We once reckoned that during the '39-'45 war Cuthbert Hall and I were out and about on evangelism with the efficient help of the catechists about two-thirds of the year. They said that never before had so much evangelistic touring been done. Like Abram and Laban, Cuthbert Hall went mostly to the north and west, Copland to the east and south. After the war, George Wells and John Towers followed on, but ultimately they were called to work in Nagpur. Where there were roads, two north, one east, one south, we could go by car or van, when there was such a vehicle. Sometimes we longed for the old days of horses, with one camp occupied and another sent ahead. For a good deal of the time off the roads, our equipment went by bullock cart, at two-and-a-half miles an hour, and we went by cycle. The aim was to make do with one cart for the whole company. It would be festooned with a tin bath, some pots and pans, some food and a surai – an evaporating pot for drinking water – a travelling altar, the magic lantern with the twelve feet square screen, gospels galore, medicine, and a small box and bedding roll for each of our helpers.

We did take sheets for bedding, and a mosquito net, but beds were not needed. It was a tradition in the villages to provide a string cot for visitors. I suppose that was demanded by lesser government officials – the grander ones would not stay in the villages but in dak bungalows. But I never availed myself of a cot. It was also a tradition to fill the tent floor with deliciously soft

Sakerwai

rice straw, and that provided sleeping accommodation for any length a person required.

Our chief medicine was for malaria, for selling as well as for ourselves. Quinine was soon out, first of supply, and then of fashion. I still have in a prayer book the Marathi word writ large – "charitra". That was the leaves we were to ask for, if we were caught out without quinine. I myself was honoured by inheriting Dr Mackenzie's little leather medicine case. It had about a dozen small phials with tablets for anything from rheumatism to rickets, diarrhoea to dysentery. They may well have been ten years old. The cholera tablets I noted were to be taken two every hour. There were ten, and they stayed with me for a long time. Then in Kothari we were taken to a man and were assured he had cholera. Who were we to question the diagnosis? I gave the relations nine of the tablets for the patient, and told them to put salt in his drinking water. Rather on the principle of keeping the last bullet for oneself or one's wife, we kept the last tablet for ourselves in case of need! The man recovered. And the last tablet was still there when we left Chanda.

On tour, it was rather fun choosing a camp site. For obvious reasons, it was well away from the outskirts of the village. As the cart approached, stones or handfuls of grass were put to mark the positions of the tent poles and the corner pegs, rather like positioning the old eighteen pounder horse-drawn guns in Cambridge. All should be set up in about five minutes.

The daily Eucharist on tour took place in some strange places – in the jungle with jungle cock or peacock joining in the Gloria, on a village school veranda, in a dak bungalow, or in the house of local Christians. Once, an undergraduate at Nagpur University, son of our revered and much respected primary school headmaster, and later himself the head of the government high school in Chandrapur, had been helping us, right out in the blue. He had to catch an early morning train on the narrow gauge railway, to get back to the university. We moved through the night, through what was reputed to be tiger jungle. I was ordered to perch on the bullock cart with a gun. I spent the night trying to keep awake, in terror not of the tiger but of dropping the gun. We reached the station long before dawn. It is well-known how thronged with people is every station in India, but here the throng was just bodies rolled in sheets: they were still asleep. Non-Christians were always excluded from the Eucharist. On this occasion, they were excluded by sleep. We moved towards the end of the platform and set up the altar. In those days, it was felt that the Eucharist, and indeed the humblest Christians too, deserved full vestments. They were in fact of linen made by my mother in Forfar. The Eucharist went forward, and we prayed for the conversion of the neighbourhood. Kamlaker returned to university life in the city, and we were grateful for his help.

At village meetings we left most of the speaking to the catechists, but in the bazaars, and before and after meetings or the magic lantern, we all spoke with individuals. One day I remember speaking to an old wifie at a bazaar. In a pause, she broke in: "Sahib, I don't understand Hindi." Nor do I. I did not let on that I had been speaking my best Pune taught Marathi, but I carried on. This time she tuned in. On another occasion, at Ghoseri or Saoli, an old grey-haired man sitting in the village street in front of his heap of saris for sale, asked me: "Sahib, tumcha dhermat dewachi oluk ho-u shakti kai?" "In your religion, can you get to know God?" The answer was Yes; it was also a challenge, to live it all the harder.

On the east side of the district, there were small irrigation canals, and each canal had a narrow cycle path along its bank. These were made of murrum, hard and smooth, though only a foot wide. Frances as a baby was once carried in a basket tied to my handlebars along such a path to Kapsi.

I used to feel a little sore at being left the magic lantern to carry. I suppose it was a case of the man saying "I can't carry this ladder by myself; I don't suppose you can?" There was the heavy brass lantern in a kerosene tin with the glass slides, the pressure lamp hanging on the other handlebar, and the screen and gospels behind.

When my wife first came to Chanda, I kindly suggested that we might move in the cool of the evening, cycling to the next dak bungalow. By moonlight, it is difficult to see detail. I had the dog on a string, and the cat in a basket on the cycle. I ran into sand, and we all collapsed gently together, man and cycle, dog and cat.

Only once did I really come to grief on a canal path. We were at Gadicurla and I had to get to a village about five miles to the south, to tell them of the Eucharist next morning. It was dark, but I had the lovely canal path and an ordinary storm lantern might give some light. I went at speed, wanting to get back for a bath and a meal. Sad to say, there was an unexplained hole in the path, about a foot wide. The wheel went in, and I went on, slithering along the gritty path on face and arms and legs, with a few glass cuts thrown in. I gave up the catechumens and turned back. When I arrived, Abdul, our cook, showed his non-Mission training, in English: "My Gaud!"

Next morning I was prevailed on to cycle to Chanda to be patched up. I was sent to the government hospital. The doctor looked me over: "You ought to have a tetanus injection." I had never had such a thing in my life. Bravely I rolled up my sleeve. "Oh, they only have them in Nagpur." I retired hurt. But my journey proved worthwhile. The

Driver's of Messers Billimoria's Store were giving a dinner party that night, and when they heard I was in Chanda they included me in their invitation. Such parties were fun – a chance of getting together with the Indian officials and their wives in the cool of the evening, often under the stars. If the women folk were in purdha, the ladies fed in another room. Often one's own servants had been asked to help and they enjoyed the outing, too. On occasion, one might even meet one's own china or cutlery!

Government officers were regularly transferred. The Drivers, like the Mission, stayed on. They were the kindest non-Christians in Chanda. As the name would make clear to some, they were Parsees. Mr Driver had been games master in the Princes' College up north. Like Dr Mackenzie, he was virtually unbeatable at tennis. Their friendship was so genuine, that it never wavered even in the dark days of the war and of nationalist feeling.

Wherever we were on tour, unless there was opposing influence abroad, the people and the children were greedy to buy gospels. That was partly, no doubt, because they were eager to exercise their skill in reading, and partly for enquiry. We always tried to tell people that they should contact Christians to discover more and we asked people why they wanted to become Christians. If it was for land, we would say we would help all we could with the government, but if they were successful, we would not let them become catechumens for some five years. If they said their mother's cousin's aunt in such and such a village was a Christian, then we knew we were on to something good. That was the best way for the faith to be spread. People would be catechumens for two years. Being so different from the Hindu custom, it was difficult for them to learn that a Christian must join in public worship every Sunday.

In their evangelistic work, the ladies of the mission were intrepid, gaily and indomitably assisted by the Biblewomen. In particular, one should mention Miss Flint and Miss Molly Mackenzie, Satywati bai, Nirmala bai Kurne and Subhakti bai. Subhakti started her adult life as a teacher, being particularly gifted in her dealings with the nursery school. Then TB struck, and things looked black. A retired Colonel in Perth had been sending us the Reader's Digest,and in it we had read of the wonders of Streptomycin. We wrote, I think it was, to the great Christian Teaching Hospital at Vellore, but they could not help. Then we tried the American forces in Bombay. They sent what was needed, and Subhakti bai got another few years of earthly life, helping the Biblewomen with great joy.

MALTI

She was reared in the shadow of All Saints Cathedral in Nagpur, a niece of one of our Padres.

Lazarus was one of our Schoolmasters. He went to the war, and became very smart in the R.I.A.S.C. Later he was captured in Malaya, and for a long time nothing was heard of him. A friendly brother claimed his provident fund. But I held on to my hope, and the fund. At last we heard he was a prisoner. I used to send him and other P.O.W.'s a quarterly card, and I still have one of his supplied by a kindly Government saying that in the care of Nippon all was well. He did come back, and married Malti.

Rumour had it that she had T.B. I remember my wife once inviting her to come into Nagpur to be examined by a Christian specialist. But she did not come. Some years later we suddenly heard that she had been ill for a month. She was very ill indeed. Out here the cost of T.B. treatment is prohibitive, and we had already appealed to Scotland for help with a T.B. teacher. It took me a few days to realise that as the wife of an ex-serviceman something might be done for her. Six copies of a letter were done out, to the D.C. (who immediately produced Rs 50), to the Red Cross in Nagpur, the Red Cross in Delhi, the Ex-serviceman's Board in Nagpur and Delhi, and the Regimental Depot. Another went to the Sanatorium.

Surprisingly enough, the Sanatorium had a bed. The Red Cross had a questionaire. And the board had a strong desire to help, but its hands were tied by the Red Cross. On we went. And meantime we did what we could to arrest the disease. Finally I went up to Nagpur. There I found the Board had a copy of the letter from the Sanatorium, accepting the patient. Confronted with this, the Red Cross said they would only act on the original – of course they were out "to help all they could, but they had to act through the proper channels." The Board sent off a wire for me asking for another letter to the Red Cross, and one to Chanda to cheer them up: "Pack and be ready."

Some days later we got a wire direct from the Sanatorium to send Malti. We had already arranged for help on the way, so off went wires to our friends. And off went poor Malti and her husband, on a more than twenty-four hours' journey in the hottest part of the year. The Anglicans failed us: probably they were on tour. Our American friends did magnificently, and were most helpful to Malti. They arrived. Then came disturbing news that her mind was deranged, and a few days later, a wire to say they had been turned out of the Sanatorium and were starting for home. There was no chance to make arrangements, but we wired our former friends, and sent a man to Wardha to watch the trains. Our own car met the midday train in Chanda, and then the Grand Trunk Express. At 10.30 p.m. we saw lights sweeping down the drive, and I went across to the hospital to welcome Malti home. We had hardly expected in that heat she would reach us alive.

Poor Malti was glad to be home. She was quite normal. The first thing she asked was that she should make her confession. I suggested that she should do it the next morning, and spent the night wondering if she would see the dawn. We were leaving for Kashmir that morning, and I suggested that Malti might like to make her confession to Canon Ohol. But she had her choice, and I went over to hear her confession at nine o'clock.

Then we left for Kashmir, and the heat of the train was nearly too much for some of us. Malti made her communion regularly, and we longed and prayed for her death. About a month later we heard that she had entered into her rest, on the very day she was to make her communion once more.

The Sanatorium is still asking for the refund of the money they advanced to send them away. The Red Cross is still promising to pay our expenses. But Malti is in peace.

Scottish Churchman, April 1952.

Later: Lazarus became a wandering Christian sadu, known only to God, wandering around India praying: हे आमच्या स्वर्गांतील पित्या, – "Our Father..." I myself in my private prayers and in my daily Matins and Evensong still pray the Lord's Prayer in Marathi. A few years later Lazarus returned home, blind. The people who had taken his house gave him food, and no doubt somewhere to sleep. Then he died.

A RELIGIOUS FAIR

Markunda Fair, one of the biggest and certainly the most central in our district, is now an established institution with us. Two years ago we had a Christian party of as many as sixteen souls, and sold something like 1600 books. Last year some of the leaders of the party failed to arrive, as two days running the crush prevented them getting a place on the train. This year the tents went off in good time, to secure our traditional place lost last year. (And be it noted that we seek not a place in the sun, but in the shade of a gigantic peepul tree, right among the crowd.)

And we went early too. Our goods and chattels had gone ahead with Stephan Master, to be sure of a place, like a king in the first class. My servant and the driver and I followed that evening in the little car. Time and place were propitious, a favourite nalla in the half-hour before dusk, and a few miles out we were lucky enough to get a peacock with No. 8 shot. But we saw nothing else. And as Lent was near we had longed to send a cheetle or sambhar back to Chanda as a sort of Shrove Tuesday pancake.

We reached Mul just before some torrential and entirely unexpected rain. (Such rain appears with strange frequency in my Markunda diary). We devoutly hoped that the rain would not put the river up and carry away the bridge. We found Stephan Master had made all the arrangements for the morrow's Eucharist for the Christians working in Mul. It was sung.

Next morning we did not get off until half-past ten. My servant and I paused as usual at the last village before Markunda, and were refreshed as usual by the patel, with a cup of milk, hot, and sugary even in these hard times of rationing and worse, out of a fine brass dish.

"Filled"

At Markunda we found that the ravages of wind and rain had

been repaired. Our henchman who looked after the tents was a thorough villager from Durgapur, father of one of our lads who had gone to war and who now has the honour of driving some high up General in Poona. Our henchman had done his work well. He had got his tents up first, and then, pleading his orders and by his own skill, he had resisted the attacks of man and weather. There we were, under the peepul tree, the envy of all the local Government officials who had deserted their own place and invaded with their tents this people's camping ground. We could afford to be gracious.

Markunda

By next morning the Fair had filled (the Marathi idiom) considerably. Bullock carts were continually arriving, with all the family and its belongings in and around, seeking a place in the crowd to stop and cook their meals and sleep. All day long, and by night as well, people came streaming in by every path and across the river. In the village street and the narrow lanes between the stalls the crowd thickened. Our day began with the Ash Wednesday Eucharist, and about twelve communicants. Then breakfast, very much in the gaze of the people, then out to the crowds. There must have been many thousands already, and still the people came. We returned for lunch at twelve, had a short rest, then out again. Tea, and out again, moving slowly through the crowds, singing bhajans in a group, then separating, shouting our wares: the Gospel of Salvation – explaining more quietly when people bought them or stopped to look at them, inviting some to meet us in Chanda, more to meet Christians in the villages, all this in the continual rush and swirl of the crowd, the creak of merry-go-rounds, and the shouts of drivers trying to get their carts through the throng, our throats made hoarse in making ourselves heard, hoarser still by the continual dust. Only occasionally do we meet with active opposition and sometimes it can be parried in a friendly way. This year we were opposed by a lawyer from Girchiroli. But I had rather spiked his guns or softened his bitterness by, quite mistakenly, greeting him as an old acquaintance at the very beginning. This strange Fair work is very different from what we usually do, though it is the same in so far as one is continually dealing with people. It is exhausting work but fascinating too, and seemingly worthwhile.

Last thing at night we had bhajans for our own mundli, with the unbelievably varied notes of the accompanying drum, and the sometimes equally unbelievable notes of the singers, all of course in the eyes and ears of the multitude. Then prayers and bed.

Impressive Crowd

Next day the programme was the same, and the crowd even bigger. The press and throng and sway of the crowd in the streets of the Fair was impressive, and to smaller people it must have sometimes been frightening. But it was a good-humoured crowd, mostly patient, and so far as our friend the sub-inspector of the police reported, honest. (One Mahar had been arrested for the crime of entering the sacred precincts of the temple.) The crowd was estimated at about 15,000.

That day a grey-haired old woman rather astonished me by walking right into my tent and greeting me as an old friend. But all was explained when she said she was one of the crowd we had welcomed into my tent one night when it rained and blew three years ago. That day, too, we met many old friends, and renewed contacts with leaders from many parts.

Finally, as I sat writing this, a man came up to my table and asked, "Is there any difference between your religion and the Hindu and the Mussalman?" From that vague beginning he moved on to an earnest and intelligent enquiry about Christianity and the Christian way of life. He turns out to be a Congress man from Gairchiroli, and in particular a follower of Tukerdave Maharaj, a religious leader of the Central Provinces. While I write, he is sitting on the rice straw on the floor of the tent, around him eight Christians in whose hands I can safely leave the cause of Christ, with an occasional word from me … And now I shall have to find some way of stopping old Stephan Master from preaching at this lone Hindu at the top of his voice without ever drawing breath …

We got to Chanda the next day, when the Fair broke up. At the river the water was in places a foot over the temporary road; later the bridges were reported to have gone, and our cartmen brought great stories of manhandling the carts, waist deep in the river. At Mul the station was literally full of people, and the line was hardly visible till the train slowly ploughed its way in. When the ticket office opened, not a minute, I fancy, before the usual time, two or three people were crushed in the crowd. Later one was reported to have died. Thousands were said to have been stranded on the far side of the river.

Meeting old friends, making new ones briefly, scattering the seed in books, and the daily Eucharist – such has been our work. Of the books, some 1500 must have gone into something like 1000 homes. We have come home weary but glad. There will be hoarse voices in church on Sunday.

Scottish Guardian, 21st March 1947.

FARTHEST NORTH

Vishranti and Samuel had only been married a few months: Vishranti, a high school girl and hostel orphan of Christian parents; Samuel, one of the first to join up and last back from Japanese hands. Theirs had been a real love match: they had not, as is usual with us, let others arrange their marriage for them. Samuel, too, was an orphan of Christian parents, and he had that sure passport to charm – Gond blood.

Not unnaturally Samuel had been a little hard to please. I think he had tried several jobs before I returned from furlough. Then at last he had got this job as a Forest Guard. And at once he had been posted to a little village right at the back of beyond.

We doubted whether he would last a month. But he did. And Vishranti was with him after the first week. We invited them to Junona, which they greatly enjoyed. There Samuel spent part of his time on his back with fever, and went back looking like death. But I never heard that he overstayed his leave. Later Vishranti had a stay in hospital. Samuel came into Chanda on duty from time to time, and it was not till Lent that I paid them my first visit.

We left in the cool of the evening, and went first to Mul. Then we struck North on the Nagpur road. At the Mul river we picnicked, most spaciously, and I felt almost in Shakespearean style.

The car was very properly drawn up at the side of the road. But when the driver protested against the soup being heated alongside the car, the fire was transferred to the middle of the road. We were not disturbed. After dinner, a hare had to be cleaned, and Manohar began to search for a stone on which to sharpen his knife. It is astounding how a small lantern increases one's blindness in the jungle, or even in open country. Manohar approached what looked like a suitable white stone, and turned away in disgust, to David our driver's loud amusement. It turned out he had sought the aid of a skull, which had escaped its funeral pyre: almost, it seemed, we were enacting the grave-diggers' scene.

From the river we made for Sindewai, the most northerly part of our District. None of us had been by road before, and as one village is very like another and Sindewai was off my map, our great fear was that we should drive right through the village and end up at Nagpur, another fifty miles beyond. However there was a magnificent signpost, and an arch of welcome left over from somebody else's reception. We drove right up to the Police Station, and found it shut.

It was now after ten o'clock, and we were somewhat concerned. Had my letter not arrived? We spotted a light in one of the quarters, and found we were expected. The Deroger, who happened to be a Christian and away in Chanda, had left orders that we were to have the choice of the Station or his house. It seemed more compliment to take the house. For me there was a bucket of water on the step. All that remained was to drag a bed out into the open.

We were in bed by eleven and up before six. En route not once did we run aground – the great danger in an Austin Seven. (The last time and the first time a tiger crossed our path, I had hit a great stone in the middle of the road and had broken the brakes. The poor tiger was probably horribly frightened by the noise, but on such an occasion it is certainly better to ruin the brakes than the back axle.) Five miles of jungle road brought us to the outskirts of Maregaon, and there was Vishranti coming out to welcome us.

The Eucharist began at seven o'clock. As there was no table in the house I built an altar of boxes. (Vishranti did murmur something about the things in the boxes, but it was only afterwards that I discovered that under the altar were buried not the bones of a saint but the prayer books of the house.) Round the altar played a dozen charming chicks, while their mother was tethered in a corner. Samuel and Vishranti appreciated having the Eucharist in their home. It proved to be a spacious two-roomed mud house, with big verandas and the roof-tree at least fifteen feet high. Afterwards we had breakfast and lunch with them. I was glad to find that Samuel liked the village people and seemed to be respected by them. His forest "parish" is about fifteen miles by ten.

Finally we set off towards Mul, in high hopes and with clear orders to get some shikar for the next day, which was refreshment Sunday. Sad to say, we got nothing.

Scottish Guardian, 11th April 1947.

THE FAR EAST

Up to date, none of us has been much east of the Waingunga at Girchiroli, and that is only forty-five miles from Chanda. For some days, Nagpur had been figuring in the paper as the hottest place in India, and we can usually flatter ourselves that we are two degrees hotter. Government had been kind in the matter of petrol coupons. The usual evangelistic work is ordinarily at a low ebb in such weather, and it seemed a fitting opportunity to go and spy out the land.

We travelled when possible, by night, and it was almost fresh sitting on top of the car at 30 m.p.h. after dark. At Mul we had a meal, and then pushed on to Sindewai where we took to the jungle. We picked up a hare on the road, and arrived at Maregaon about half-past nine. They were all awake and expecting us, the forest guard and his wife and her brothers and sister whom we had sent out for the holidays. We had family prayers, and quickly got down to sleep.

Next morning we were up with the dawn about five, and I had a glorious swim in the tank not two hundred yards from the house. Then followed the Sung Eucharist, with, I think, twelve in the congregation, and a delicious breakfast. An Inspector of police had been killed two days before when his car fell down the canal bank in those parts, so we eschewed the bank and took the low road through the forest to Kheiri, a little bungalow standing right above another irrigation tank. There I bathed and bathed and bathed while the Chaukidar was being fetched to open the bungalow. Promode Master and Bajerao Master were with me, and they proposed cycling next day to Gunjewai and Vihad, while I returned to show the Magic Lantern at Maregaon and give them another celebration. So in the evening David and Abdul and I returned, and as the Petromax wouldn't work, we did our best with a light from the car. Next morning we were off by eight, and went a little out of our way to visit the Guard's sister, who had just finished her Teacher's training and was taking part in the Government Adult Education campaign.

A Tussle

We found Premla alone, as we had been told she was, among half a dozen men. They had made excellent arrangements, but we said she would retire to Maregaon and start adult education there, until they could find her a companion. The District Inspector was in the offing, and I was asked to face him. He insisted on showing me all the excellent arrangements he had made. I praised them all, and returned to my point that Premla must have a companion or return with us. "But that will upset all our plans." "I know it will. And I am very sorry, but that does not matter at all, in comparison with the honour of women." – a phrase we often read out here. Then I played the ace of trumps: "Mr Ghandi was quite insistent on that." Very well, the wife of one of the masters would stay with our girl. She proved to be eighteen, and we thought that perhaps she might not quite fulfil our purpose. Then the inspector produced an old woman from the village: she would act as chaperone. We thought it at least wise to hear what she herself had to say, and when rather hesitatingly the old woman had agreed, we left Premla with instructions to pack up and make tracks for Maregaon the first night the old woman failed to turn up. And as we went, we had time to renew our admiration for the arrangements that had been made.

If It Rains Come Back

What was left of that day we spent at Vihad, and gave them a celebration the next morning. Then we were off to the Sunday bazaar at Garchiroli, selling gospels and other books all the afternoon. Next morning we had a celebration for the sub-inspector of police and his family, and moved on into what was terra incognita. The deroga's family were kindness itself, and the rich meal they served us proved too much for one of the servants. The deroga insisted on calling for more petrol from Chanda. And his parting advice was ominous: "Start back at once if it rains."

The mud road quickly took to the forest. There was forest and more forest, with an occasional village in the middle of a great sea of rice fields, then forest and bigger forest. The road was atrocious. We had been told something about the first ten miles of it, but I couldn't remember whether it was the worst bit or the best. We found ourselves climbing slightly, right on top of a wooded ridge, with wooded hills in the neighbourhood and frequent nallas that would fill up when it rained. We came to the big village of Dhanora, and went on another fifteen miles to Murumgaon. There we halted, within ten miles of the eastern edge of Chanda District.

The village was on the Gond pattern, with houses widely spaced apart. And the houses seemed spotlessly clean, with mud plaster of different colours inside and out, and strange, crude decorations that were entirely new to us on the walls. The people were friendly, talking Marathi, Hindi, Gondi, and Chatisgarri, and between us we managed to make ourselves understood pretty well. Those who could read were very keen to buy books in Hindi or Marathi. The weekly bazaar was comparatively small and proportionately homely, meeting in the shade of some mango trees on the outskirts of the village. There was obviously a good deal of drinking of the local liquor. And, unfortunately, it is tremendously potent. (In fiften years in India, never once did I taste strong drink.) At Murumgaon a great crowd gathered for the magic lantern show. Promode spoke in Hindi. The local ranee herself attended. And when we had humbly craved her permission to begin, we went ahead. Unfortunately the ranee sat so far away that she can have seen little of the pictures. Later we presented her with a gospel and some other books.

Gond Helpers

Early next morning after the Eucharist, we moved back fifteen miles to Dhanora, which proved to be rather a bigger town with a police headquarters and the seat of a zemindari. We called on the zemindar and found him a delightful old man with white locks, interesting to talk to.

The Storm

That night we had made elaborate preparations for showing the magic lantern. But the weather decreed otherwise. Just before darkness came on, I noticed a dark cloud sweeping towards us. I suggested casually that my bathwater might be carried in before the rain came. The wind got up impressively, and I jumped into the car and put it under the lee of the bungalow gable. David got in to put up the curtains, and did not get out for three-quarters of an hour. Within three minutes the storm was on us. Never have I seen such fury. Thunder there was, but it was not particularly noticeable. The lightning just showed a grey sheet of water, and everything going before the wind. It was the smashing, tearing fury of the wind and rain that was impressive. It seemed that it would sweep all before it. I thought of the tale of the ill-fated bungalow at Chimur where the D.S.P. had spent a night in the shelter of the bare walls, after the roof had been stripped, and said Evensong.

The bungalow was right in the middle of some mango trees. Every now and then there was a terrific crash, and I could hardly tell whether it was a storm driven mango striking the tiles, or the fall of a tree. When the storm had blown itself out in little over half an hour, there were thousands of mangos on the ground. Our people took what they wanted. Then a crowd of Mahar boys arrived with baskets, and we thought it might be a little hard on the owners if they took everything. But the boys convinced us that their fathers owned the trees, and we helped them with lanterns. Soon all was still except for the steady hissing of the wet ground.

The Map

The storm had given us a holiday, and I sat thinking of our strategy. In the early days Christianity went, I believe, along the Roman roads and the trade routes. It seems to be going much the same way with us. Near the western side of the District there is a main road running north and south for some 200 miles. And on that road Christianity seems to be established and growing: Bhandak, Ghorpeth, Chanda, Bellarshah, Ahiri, Sironcha and their neighbouring villages have all got their congregations. From Chanda there is this other road running east for about 100 miles, and on that too, there is at least hope of growth: Mul, Gadicurla, Vihad, the witness of the police at Girchiroli. And now we are looking to the boundary.

Europeans

As I mused I longed for Christians in every village along that road, to spread the gospel throughout the country. And I thought longingly of what I heard of the strength of the Church in St. John's Diocese in Africa. Our area is just over half that of St. John's Diocese. What could we not do, I muse, with half their number of Christians (Although admittedly not every Christian is a good advertisement for Christ.)

In Chanda district we have at present only one European outside the Mission. I knew there were many in Africa, and Crockford now feeds my envy by telling me there are 17,000 Europeans in St. John's Diocese. What a potential help for evangelism and witness half that number would be. But we have to deal with things as they are, and go ahead.

And did not Christianity also spread with the Roman army? I found comfort in that thought, for we seem to have a chance of spreading in a somewhat similar way. In the last ten years, some dozen of our Christian young men have gone into the local police force, and sooner or later they will find themselves with their families in the twenty-two scattered stations of the District. That way, too, Christianity is shown to the world, and sometimes very impressively.

But the storm was over, and it was cool to sleep.

Next morning at five o'clock I was saying Matins on the veranda when some women arrived to take the gleanings: but there was little left, and the only signs of the storm were fallen branches and broken trees. None of the trees had come up by the roots, I suppose because the ground was hard, but several had broken right over. That morning the two boys who had been looking after the lantern sheet brought it in and laid it at our feet, muddy and in shreds, rather like the remains of Joseph's coat, or an ear that has been rescued out of the mouth of the lion.

The road was dry, but the dust was laid, as we made our way back to Girchiroli. There were black buck in the bed of the Waingunga. On we went to Vihad and Mul and Gadicurla, and once more to Chanda.

Scottish Guardian, 1 July 1949.

BAPTISED IN THE VILLAGE TANK

Baptism at Ghorpeth

Experienced missionaries have often said that Christian converts should be encouraged to bring in their relations, that this is a most fruitful method of extending the Church, and that the fullest use should be made of this method.

An example of this method in operation has just been seen in Chanda. In the first week of January a Mahar family, father and mother and two children, were baptised in the "tank" (i.e. the village pond) at Junona. And about three weeks later, a young married couple, two widows and three children (Mahars again) were baptised in the pond at Ghorpeth. All these folk were related to a large Christian family in Chanda. And old Mr. and Mrs. Jacob Ramteke (the parents of Wasant, Samuel, Madhuker, etc.) and Mrs. Ramteke's widowed sister Tamabai (until recently the only Christian woman in Ghorpeth) have been largely responsible, under God, for bringing in these relations of theirs into the fold of the Church. How exactly they are all related to each other is far too complicated a question to go into here. The thing that matters is that here we see the Christian Church growing along family lines.

The Ghorpeth baptism will be talked about in the village for many days to come. At half-past six on the morning of Friday, January 28th, the Mission van set off from Chanda to do the eleven-mile run northwards along the Warora road. We had a full load including, besides the entire mission staff, two catechists and three Biblewomen (who had been instructing the catechumens for over a year past), and various Christian relations. We also had with us a young Oxford graduate, who has recently joined the staff of St. Paul's School, Darjeeling, and who has been spending part of his cold weather holiday in Chanda. He was appointed press photographer for the occasion. We reached Ghorpeth at about 7 o'clock. Mr. Jagtap and Joseph Master had already arrived from Bhandak, six miles further along the road. (The new Christians will be part of Mr. Jagtap's parish). We found the candidates gathered outside Tamabai's house. It was a beautiful, fresh morning; the sun had only just risen and there was quite a nip in the air. The thought of immersion in the village tank at this early hour was somewhat alarming to some of the candidates, and timid overtures were made to Mr. Copland in favour of holding it in somebody's house, under warmer, and less public, conditions. This suggestion was sternly brushed aside, and preparations for the procession were quickly completed.

At 7.15 we set off from the village to the tank; Nilkant in front, carrying a twelve-foot bamboo cross, followed by Mr. Jagtap and Mr. Copland, Mr. Towers and myself, and then the candidates, escorted by their Christian relations, with the Biblewomen and the "Memsahibs" bringing up the rear. Behind came a motley crowd of villagers, who were warmly invited to come and watch the ceremony. The tank was a bare quarter of a mile from the village, just off the main road. This gave us time to sing through the hymn "Khrist mazha Tarenara" (Christ is my Saviour) about half a dozen times. Halfway there we were joined by the catechists, who had gone ahead to put up a small tent to be used as a changing room. By the time we reached the chosen spot on the bank of the pond, there must have been sixty people present. Mr Copland stood in front, near the edge of the water: facing him stood the candidates, flanked by their sponsors; and to one side stood the curious onlookers from the village. On the top of the bank behind stood Nilkant, holding the bamboo cross. All round us were the fields of ripening "juwar", looking beautifully fresh and green in the early morning sun.

The service, conducted by Mr. Copland, followed the order prescribed in the Prayer Book for the "Baptism of such as are of Riper Years". When the central moment came, Mr. Copland girded up his cassock and stepped down into the water, leading Prelad, Tamabai's married son, by the hand. With the water well above his knees, Mr. Copland turned to Stephen Master to enquire the candidates Christian name. "John," came the answer. And then John Prelad was three times dipped beneath the water, "In the name of the Father, and of the Son and of the Holy Ghost." Thus cleansed and reborn in Christ, he was led back to the little congregation on the bank. "We receive this person into the congregation of Christ's flock, and do sign him with the sign of the cross ..." Next came Chandrabhaga, John's young wife; then Vimal Ramabai and her two children, a girl of twelve and a boy of ten; and lastly Martha Sarzabai and her little girl of ten. As soon as they had been baptised, they each disappeared for a few moments into the tent behind the bank; and returned in their best clean clothes. It was indeed a joyful occasion. As we said the Lord's prayer together at the end, we felt we were all a united family. These new Christians had not only been united more closely than ever before with their own Christian relations; they had also been brought into the family of Christ's Church; they were now our brothers and sisters in Christ.

After kneeling for the final blessings, we set off again in procession; in the same order as before, except that this time the cross was carried by John Prelad, newly become a Christian.

G.R. Wells, Scottish Guardian, 25th March 1949.

MOHOURLIE'S FIRST EASTER

We had been out to Mohourlie every week in Lent, for a Eucharist and instruction. The first Christians had not long been baptised and had been confirmed on Mothering Sunday. They were fully informed of the necessity of coming at crack of dawn on Easter Day, so that I could get back to Durgapur to help. To our surprise, and to the credit of all those concerned, the three families turned up on time.

The thermometer was 110 in the shade. Holy Saturday had been busy, with the last of hostel confessions and various arrangements to be made. A message came from the Range Office of Mohourlie, begging for a lift in the van. The van was packed, not forgetting Easter cards from Scotland, and the family set off about 5 p.m. when the worst of the heat was over. Officially we could not stay at the Forest Bungalow, as it was occupied by an American shikari trying to bag his first tiger. But he was being shown the ropes by the Nawab of Porla, a great friend of the Mission. Away back in the 1870's the Reverend Israel Jacob recorded a visit to the Nawab of Porla, and his successor is still our friend, and sends his son to Bishop Cotton School in Nagpur. He and the American had invited us to dinner, and had promised to put us up.

As was to be expected, the Range Officer brought two or three camp followers with him, and a bag of wheat that spilt all over the floor. At last we were off, and somewhere beyond Durgapur one of the Forest subordinates suggested that I couldn't really shoot from the inside of the car. It was agreed that I should sit on top.

Horns In The Thicket

It looked as though we were to have an uneventful trip, if rocking and rolling over one of the worst roads in Chanda can be called uneventful. (Only the other day, one of us had his eye bunged up by a load of bamboos that swung around and knocked him off his bicycle.) Then as we neared Mohourlie, I spotted a fine head showing above the undergrowth. When the car had been brought to a standstill, I reported a cheetle stag, and asked if it was to be shot. The Ranger approved, the car moved back and I got a shot at the stag. There was a click instead of the usual blinding cloud of flame and smoke: a misfire. I tried again. But by that time the stag was moving back too. There was a great clatter from the tin roof, as I moved about to get a clear view of him. Finally I found myself balancing on the string cot tied to the roof, and the rifle barrel waving round in circles. The cot and the barrel steadied, and all was lost in a cloud of smoke. By the sound of things we had our Easter feast. Remembering a previous occasion when I had shot too well, and the Ranger had missed his chance to "halal" a sambhar, I called at once for a knife. But none was available. I offered to unearth my razor blade, but that reminded our driver he had a blade in his pocket. With that unlikely weapon, the needful deed was done.

Mohourlie gave us a most friendly welcome. We found a luxurious tent made ready for us, though, of course, we slept in the open. The children were put to bed, and after a short chat we went in to dine. The Nawab seemed to have brought a party of friends with him, and we sat down ten to dinner. As the only woman present, my wife was set at the head of the table. The Nawab proved a perfect host, and we had a delightful meal. Soon afterwards, two Jeeps went off to look for the tiger, and we went off to bed.

The Church Universal

"The Lord is risen." "The Lord is risen indeed. Alleluia!" On Easter morning we were early astir; I suppose about 5 a.m. The blue-lined bathroom of the tent made a charming apse. The travelling altar was a gift from Peterborough, now much blended with Chanda teak; the fair linen a gift from Forfar, the vestments from Tillyrie. The Sursum Corda was the same as ever; the rest of the Eucharist was sung to Indian music. Glorious sweet-smelling "champa" flowers were strewn on the altar; the lights were provided by local oil and raw cotton from the fields in the lids of Paludrine tins. There we all knelt in the rice straw, to greet the risen Lord.

That huge American had flown thousands of miles and landed in our midst. It was impressive to see him kneeling there among our friends. He was deaf, heard little and perhaps understood less; but he made up for it all by a most benign smile. There must have been a dozen Christians from Mohourlie, Chanda was represented, and Durgapur, Scotland and England and America. Some of us were united by race, others by language. But only in our Baptism and in the Communion were we one.

Easter had come to Mohourlie.

WHEELS AGAINST THE SUN

"The sun will soon be down, and if we are not careful, you will be spending the night in the jungle: if it comes off again, you will have to go back."

We had crossed the Waingunga by boat, and had done the seven miles to Girchiroli without mishap. But now, in spite of tightening it and in spite of all the sand we'd thrown on it, Jaiwant's chain had come off for the sixth time in half a mile. So our prospective master had to be left behind.

On the banks of the Wainganga,
David our driver

Another half-mile and there was a grinding crunch, and Anand Master's back wheel was jammed. He suspected a broken axle. I took the map and left him, with orders for him to join me or hunt for me next morning.

Already it was getting ominously cool. It was now a race against the sun. I had about seven miles of unknown jungle ahead of me, and forty minutes to sundown. Another half-mile, and I struck into the forest, with villagers shouting directions as I went.

I had to find my own way to Jamri, where the young zemindar had lately asked the Mission to provide a master – a fruit of our summer tour to the east and of a Christian deroger at Girchiroli. It was worth trying to get there that day, for we only had time for a brief visit before the end of the year.

The road forked and the map was uncertain, but there was no time to explore. I left an arrow in the sand – duly noted on the morrow – and pressed on. The road narrowed and the trees closed in, but it was too late to turn back. I had the inch-to-the-mile map clutched in greasy fingers, and it suggested that the road could not take me far wrong in any case. (Experience whispered otherwise.) At any rate I could still ride. Where the road was sand, mindful of the babes in the wood, I tore leaves from the trees and dropped them as I lurched and skidded through.

Next it was my own bicycle that went wrong, and a pedal broke loose. But it slipped on again, and stayed on most of the time. At last I came to a clearing, but the rice fields were cut and there was no-one about. Then came jungle again, and another clearing, and then smoke, then voices, and I was suddenly in the middle of a crowd of cattle coming home for the night.

"What village is this?"

"Chandala."

So it had been the wrong road, but the map had been right.

"Is this the road to Jamri?"

"Yes. Not far."

So on I rattled and plunged.

On such occasions, the rule is to follow not the cart-track, but the path worn smooth by bare feet. Soon I met half a dozen Gonds. "Jamri?" "Not far." It was almost dark when I came out of the high grass into another clearing, and there almost a mile away on the far side hung the smoke of evening cooking. If it was not Jamri, I would take a guide from there.

Jamri it was. And in front of the biggest house in the dusk I found a young man sitting with some grey-beards.

"Are you the Zemindar Sahib?"

"Yes."

None of our letters had arrived, and my visit was wholly unexpected. But they were quite unperturbed, and made me very welcome.

A Dhiver was hailed to cook for me, and a cock was called for. "Did my religion demand that I should cut its head off with my own hand?" No, that was quite immaterial. (I doubted whether I could even have wrung its neck decently.)

We sat chatting of "this and that" and came round to the school. "The arrangement we made yesterday cancelled zhalla," said the zemindar to the company. It was amusing to hear the English word right out in the Jungle. And apparently we were only just in time. They would show us the proposed site for the school they would build, and the master's house, and the land they would give us to-morrow. Like the perfect host he was, the zemindar would touch nothing till my meal was ready.

I had Bishop Wood's sleeping bag with me, and that night I was glad of its warmth. Next morning, sad to say, there was no congregation for a Eucharist, so I let them take me out shooting. We saw nothing, except at times literally a wall of grass swaying down as the buffaloes pushed through it.

When we got back three hours later, my men were there. They had come on foot to the village at the edge of the jungle, now also offering a school, and had spent the night there. We approved the Jamri plans, and changed them slightly. The zemindar proved a good swimmer, and we had a delightful bathe in the tank, where the village women washed their clothes, whose water had so refreshed me the night before.

We stayed another night to get better acquainted. The Maria and Raj Gonds produced some genuine and very vivid village entertainment in their different styles. At midnight, distributing graceful praise around, I retired on to the veranda, and went to sleep. When I awoke, all had gone, and the moonlit world was strangely quiet.

Next morning Jamri had its first Eucharist, and we sped away. We preached in the village at the jungle's edge, lunched at Girchiroli, and missed the 'bus at the Waingunga. We chased it and missed it again at Vihad, and the Towers gave me tea. From there we got a lift for seven miles in a lorry, and cycled to Mul. Finally a Nagpur 'bus raced us quickly home, unexpectedly early by nine o'clock at night.

Metaphorically, we had secured a footing, but there is still much to be done before the school is opened.

Scottish Guardian, 30 December 1949.

RETREATS

Under Dr Mackenzie and Mr Treble, and no doubt long before, there had been quiet days for all sorts of people. Before our time, these became one night retreats, and they were a great refreshment to the body as well as soul, and particularly to the hard-working village women. One could rely on the thoughtful preparation of addresses. Amusingly, at the actual time of the retreat, the cooking was the chief concern. And it was the men who were liable to be critical. The men and boys slept in tents, and to the number of twenty or so, they fed in the disused open-sided carpenters' shop. The women, of course, and the girls, were in the women's compound.

Not many of the grown-ups made their confession, but most of the boys and girls did. Usually we found the conductor among our own priests, Indian or European. Also we had the Indian Archdeacon of Nasik, and Canon Ohol of that Diocese, Archdeacon Batty, and the Bishop of Nasik. We were very fortunate in having the Wantage Sisters and the Cowley Fathers in Pune (Poona), speaking our own Marathi. On different occasions we had Fr Williams SSJE, and Fr Huntly.

In Chanda we were not accustomed to incense in church. So when Fr Huntly was coming, we made a thurible most effectively out of a cigarette tin. (That dates it: where would you find a cigarette tin today?)

Cigarettes even in those days could be a problem. Cuthbert Hall's main area for evangelism was to the north of Chanda city. The Wardha river was the boundary of our district. Once, when camping near the river, Cuthbert saw some workers of the neighbouring American mission on the other side. Hospitably, he invited them over and hospitably, he offered a cigarette before lighting up himself. In a few days a stern letter came from the head of one mission to the other head, in effect: "If your workers want to go to the Devil with cigarettes, please ask them not to try and take ours with them."

And that was not the end. Later we had the same American over for some lecture or course. Our ladies were quite exhausted arranging the catering – my wife, Molly Mackenzie, and I think Helen Wells. Flopping down on the sofa, one of them exclaimed: "Let's have a cigarette!" That was probably the only one they would have in a year. They lit up, and in a moment in came our American friend. There was an embarrassed silence. I don't think any of the three had the inspiration to throw a faint.

Fr Huntly recorded his impressions in the Cowley Evangelist 1950. I don't know if he smoked, but he seemed to have welcomed the cigarette tin: "CHANDA: As you see, I am staying at this splendid Mission. I have come to take three retreats, one of men. That is over. There were thirty men in it. The second has just finished for women, and mostly teachers. The third one begins this evening for illiterate village women. I am enjoying my stay here. It is an excellent Mission. All the priests and wives and workers are keen and work like a team. They have an excellent standing with the people; they are all friends, not the big missionary father-and-mother stuff. It is a joy to see it all. The older missionaries who have gone have laid a solid foundation. Of course, there is no other Mission here and that makes for a united, happy family. The missionaries serve the men and women at meals and there is a real atmosphere of mutual trust and friendliness. I have learnt a few wrinkles from them."

For British readers it should perhaps be explained that the description "illiterate" is in no way condemnatory, as it would tend to be in this country. The women may have been holy, leaders in their community, most knowledgeable and capable, but they had not had the opportunity of learning to read.

INDIAN MUSIC

When first going to India in 1938, I heard some Indian singing on board ship, and made the horrible mistake of thinking they were making fun of plainsong. Quickly Cuthbert Hall and I were won over to it.

So far as I know, there is nothing like the bhajan in Europe. It is popular music, gloriously and delightfully popular, known and loved and enjoyed, not by one age group but by all, from the smallest boy in a skimpy shirt herding the cattle, to the grey-head, and of course by the women and girls as well. Usually one line is sung solo, then it is repeated by all, often accompanied by the rhythm and music of the tabla, the small Indian hand drum. I suppose the subject is usually religious. The tunes are as traditional as the air the people breathe. Before starting, the drums are warmed over a fire of straw. When all is tuned, the singing begins and goes on well into the night. The men sit around in the open air, so the singing and drumming carries far.

Because the music is known and accepted by all, the bhajan is a magnificent instrument for evangelism. Waman Ramteke, one of the younger catechists, and now ordained, was an adept at this kind of preaching. Well do I remember Waman, in a rather plaintive voice, singing "Mali dada ..." "O Mr Gardiner, where is He put?". Then Waman would swing into the quicker "Khrista mazha taranara ..." "Christ, my Saviour ...", and half the world would join in. Again, because the bhajan is so generally understood and accepted by all, a bhajan mandli, a singing group, was often formed in a congregation for pleasure and for evangelism. St Thomas in Nagpur was, I think, the first to go ahead with such evangelism in our parts. They used to come to Mul, some 30 miles east of Chandrapur, for a week of evangelism. The younger men and girls of Chanda followed suit among the nearer villages, and so did Durgapur. We were all, of course, made well aware of the former Bishop Azariah of Dornikal and his dictum: each congregation is responsible for missionary work for five miles around.

Long ago, the Revd Haberjee Bhalerao had produced our Marathi hymn book, with tunes Indian and Western. Some of the words were written by Shanti bai Dhandeker, a Chanda poetess. Mr Bhalerao was the grand old man of Chanda Christians in our day, and parish priest, ripe in years and experience and wisdom. When Cuthbert Hall and I wanted to introduce the tabla into Church music, he said no: it was too much associated with heathen Hindu things. We accepted that he was right. But later on, with a younger generation, the tabla was readily accepted in church.

In the old days, the Eucharist in St Andrew's in Chanda was sung to Merbecke. In Pune, the Wantage Sisters were naturally Marathi speakers. We learned that Sister May had produced two settings for the Eucharist to Indian Music. Most kindly, Sister May came to stay and to teach us. Gradually our Christian worship was becoming more and more fully Indian.

Ladies' bungalow

ACCOUNTS

This is about financial, not evangelistic, accounts. The Head of the Mission had a tiny office at one end of the bungalow veranda. This was just a sun trap, or a roasting oven. Ruben Master in his accounting capacity had a similar sun trap at the other end. Did that contribute to our keenness to get out on evangelistic touring? There was a safe in each office.

On the income side in our time, I suppose we had about £4,500 a year from Scotland, plus extras from the CWMA and elsewhere. I think all teachers in schools were paid from government grants to the Mission – perhaps six to eight schools at any one time, with twenty or so teachers. There would be some income from the Hospital, with four nurses or so to pay, and from the hostels. There were three or four Biblewomen, four or five catechists, half a dozen priests, Indian and European, and two, three or four lady workers, including the Indian doctor and up to eighty children to be fed in the hostels. Before the war there were market-garden workers, a building gang, and carpenters.

Actually, getting hands on the cash was quite a tour de force. There was no bank in Chanda. One of us had to go to the Imperial Bank in Nagpur. That meant a free trip, leaving I suppose about 6 a.m., finding lunch with the Bishop and Mrs Hardy or the Marrisons of the Church Army, the Mure Hospital and St Ursula's School, or Sir Geoffrey Burton of the ICS and Lady Burton – all very kind and welcoming friends. I can't think how we moved about the big distances in Nagpur.

Those were the days of solid rupees, and we needed lots of change. Did one really have to hear each single rupee ringing true as it dropped on the stone floor? Certainly that was the way we paid them out. But the five rupees came in new packets of clean notes: that was compensation.

Later, with the march of progress and history, our free jaunts to Nagpur ended, the National Bank of India came to Chanda, and crisp rupee notes came in welcome packets of a hundred.

The head of each institution, or a deputy, would come in on pay-day to collect the cash. That provided a welcome chance of meeting friends and for having a chat with the Head of the Mission.

Mr Treble had set a fine example in keeping the accounts and in personally balancing them at the end of each month. I felt this tied one too much to the centre, so I kept the safe key and Ruben Master kept the accounts and dealt with day to day cash. At the end of the year we had a very grand Hindu auditor from Nagpur. If at the audit there were two or three annas unaccounted for, I felt it was a good use of cash to keep the auditor for an extra day and let him chase the truant annas. The deep discussions about such missing annas always amused me, however proper it was. I fancy Bishop Wood did things in much the same way.

The return journeys from Nagpur could be entertaining. One would stroll along the train to see if any government bigwig from Nagpur had on a special coach. One would drop in for a chat, and then return to one's humbler place at the next stop. The trip might be rewarded with one of those delicious curries handed in on a tray at a wayside station, with half-a-dozen little pots of etceteras. And always at the season, one would return with a huge basket of luscious Nagpur oranges to be shared out among the bungalows. The oranges were mostly green, their thick skins almost fell away when you looked at them: they were undoubtedly one of the luxuries of life in Chanda, and they were astoundingly cheap.

On one of those early morning journeys to Nagpur, I remember chatting to a railway engineer in his special coach alongside the express. He very kindly offered me a cup of tea. Just then the whistle went, and the train started moving. "Hold on, Tommy: the Padre hasn't finished his tea." So the driver put on the brakes, and the great Grand Trunk Express to Delhi waited while the missionary humbly gulped his tea.

Oranges were Chanda luxuries. There were others that may be worth mentioning. The hot weather was pretty awful. When you got a clean cassock out of the cupboard, it felt as if it had just been ironed. But the Club, only a quarter of a mile away, had what was probably an old Gond bath, measuring about twenty feet by ten feet by six feet, shaded and roofed over. I used to cycle there about 3 p.m.: it was gloriously refreshing. Naturally, the water evaporated. When it had got to three feet and I had skinned my nose on the bottom, I thought it was time to give up my lonely bathe. The khuskus was another hot weather luxury. This is a bamboo frame made to fit in a doorway, and thatched with grass. By the old style, a punkhawallah threw water on the grass from the outside. Of course he fell asleep from time to time. An improvement was self-help, throwing water on the grass from the inside. Then lying on a half inch mattress on the stone floor, every now and again there was a vestige of a cool breath of air: while it lasted, that was heaven on earth. Later we joined the march of progress: when electricity had come, we made a window khuskus about three feet by three feet by three feet, with a water tank on top dripping on the grass continuously, and with a fan inside facing inwards. That too was good.

UPLIFT

Today, someone might be excused for thinking that the missionary work of the Church – in Britain or overseas – was mainly concerned with material things – with food and small industry and so forth. We had, I suppose, just as much concern: we called it village uplift. But in our day that was not all our work. God certainly had made body as well soul, but we had been sent specially to preach, teach, baptize. Others as well as ourselves, were concerned with bodily and material welfare.

Alex Wood took on 250-300 orphans, and that entailed keeping as many alive as possible, and then teaching and training those who survived. And what good results he had! There was Ruben Master, the trusted right-hand man of several Heads of the Mission, and Stephen Master the devoted catechist, both serving in '14-'18 war; there was Monica bai, good mother to the hostel girls, and the mother of the first Chanda Bishop, Arthur Luther; Habel Jagtap, devoted parish priest and father-in-law of our second Chanda bishop; and Simon Master, imperturbable headmaster, Christian example to us all, and father of one of the first men to go to university and later distinguished headmaster of the huge government high school in Chanda. Probably there were others as distinguished but unknown as original orphans.

Dr K W Mackenzie built a tank at Durgapur, no doubt with a government grant and local voluntary labour. The result was improved irrigation for the crops. Inspiration, I think, must often have come to us from the National Christian Council (NCC) REVIEW. With cement work we were also helped by technical papers from the collieries – by the Moores in particular. How many readers know that bamboo can be useful for reinforcement? Honey was once the "in word", a simple way of improving village health. Bees, of course, were in plentiful supply in the jungle. We had a hive carefully made according to the plan supplied, in the only wood available – the best of teak. Example is the best teaching: we would show the way for others. If a Gond could face a tiger with his little axe, he could face a thousand bees with only his loin-cloth. It was a fearsome sight. We got a Gond to climb a tree and collect the bees. I can still see him, up a tree in the middle of a milling cloud of bees, pausing now and again to brush them off his thighs and chest. Somehow he got them, and we got them into the hive. I had no experience to look back to: I had no experience at all. Delegation is always good; I delegated my authority and the bees to the ladies' bungalow. All went well for a time. Then one day by accident or design, someone left the bees shut in all day. The sun did the rest and the experiment was over.

Pachmarhi was the semi hill station of the Central Provinces. There, amusingly, instead of going up into the hills to get cool, one went down into a deep gorge. In the church there is a memorial to an officer who was stung to death by bees – and his horse with him. So there are other bees and fiercer, as Kipling readers know. Kipling's bees were only a bit north of Chanda, on our Markunda's Waingunga. We saw them first, or thought we saw them, on our very first visit to Markunda Fair. We had arrived at night and we had no idea where to camp. Near the temple was a colossal peepul tree. There were people sleeping all around, but under the tree there was space that would be shaded – just the place for us. Next morning when we looked up, we saw huge bunches of bees and honey, hanging from different branches. That year the bees were kind. Next year by early arrival, we came again under the bees, and the tradition was established. That was the Christians' place and always the bees were kind.

Malaria was then the curse of our district, though it was weeded out later. It was discovered that a fish the size of a minnow loved the larvae. Any forward looking outfit would, of course, nourish and share out the gambusia. We did. On a visit to Nagpur, I found the right government office, and was sent to some public gardens. I got hold of a large tin and some thirty or forty gambusia and nursed them in the Grand Trunk to Chanda, like a boy with his holiday minnows. Thereafter they were carefully shared out among wells and tanks. Unless they died off when DDT took over, I have no doubt their descendants are enjoying rare larvae to this day. To combat malaria and teach good ways, we provided small head nets for the hostels – a mixed blessing, as it was felt they restricted any breeze that might come. In 1970 when we returned to Chandrapur, we were astounded to find that nets were not needed. Long may that last!

In the Nilgaries, one sometimes smelt a refreshing boiling of eucalyptus leaves from miles away, just as in Chanda there was sometimes a delicious smell of sugar-cane juice being boiled in the open, in a pan about eight feet across and eight inches deep. The Mission had the distinction of introducing the eucalyptus tree to the district. There are hundreds of different kinds, and it may be that we did not get the most suitable but several survived and grew. Today there are millions in the jungle, planted for quickly grown timber and probably for the paper works. I expect the leaves are used as well. The Streatfeild family took over running the centuries old Gond garden in what was the Mission compound, as an example for the surrounding countryside. They are leading the villages in agricultural improvements. Of course, they take their full share in the worshipping life of the Chandrapur congregation.

Making bore hole latrines

It was Dr Mackenzie who got the apparatus for making bore hole latrines. This was an advance which was greatly appreciated. It was a great thing to have a latrine at the bottom of the garden, instead of having to go to the rather smelly out-skirts of the village. The gouge was, I suppose, about nine inches in diameter; a rod was attached, with a cross bar for the man-power to twist it. Extra pieces were fitted to the rod as the hole went down.

We in Chanda never went in for tube wells, possibly because the apparatus would be too expensive, more probably because the villages had good wells, and they seldom went dry. Before our time, a windmill and pipes had taken water from the compound well to the girls' hostel; but that had fallen into disrepair. Today, I believe all Chandrapur has piped water. Towards the end of our time we got electricity in the Mission compound.

Around 1938 Dr Mackenzie scored another first with septic tanks. He provided one for the bungalow servants and their families. I followed on, gaining specialist knowledge of u-bends and all the rest. We provided tanks for the hostels, and for every bathroom in every bungalow. Shortly before we left Chandrapur, Mr Hastak, the leading lawyer in the city, a Brahmin, and a doughty though charming opponent of Christianity, asked if he could come and see me. Was this it? He dressed with distinction, and always wore the traditional cerise hat, with a sort of cockscombe on top. I thought it polite to go and see him. When I arrived, Mr. Hastak said he had heard of our septic tanks: would I explain to him how one should be built?

Even the hospital was provided with septic tanks. But would they be used? "You can't ask nurses to do the work of sweepers and carry about bedpans! They will go on strike." Thanks to the courage and loyalty of Sharada bai, the senior nurse, and thanks to the tact and example of Mrs Copland, the tanks won the day, and the sweepers lost their jobs. (There was a whisper of a change of practice after our time, but I don't know about that.) Now the hospital building is part of a big Christian English-medium school.

In Bishop Wood's time, the Mission had scored a first with the first Scout troop in India. The Guides followed with the first company in the Central Provinces. And Miss Molly Mackenzie (later Mrs Hall) scored another first of some kind with our nursery school. The Baden-Powells once visited Bishop Wood and the Scouts in Nagpur.

We set an example, too, by growing bananas on the soak pits for bath water, though sometimes they had to share space with the fragrant frangipani.

Dr Mackenzie was a great gardener, and we all followed on. We showed how easy it was to grow papaya – paw paws to some. We discovered that the seeds had a good spicy taste and that they provided some vitamin or other.

The inspiration for this must have come from the SPCK Annual Report. I had been a member since ordination, and my father before me. The Mission organised the first book fair in India. ISPCK was most helpful.

The idea was to get together hundreds of books, as there was no good bookshop in the district. There was to be general literature, religious books, popular specialist subjects, and so on and so on, in English and Marathi, and some in Hindi as well. The big problem was to get the people to come: they would certainly buy if they did. Neighbouring towns were invited, headmasters were interviewed or informed, government officers were told. The DC would open the fair. And the place? The Mission was rather outside the city. We heard there was a town hall. We found it and hired it, and placarded it, and festooned it with bunting. On the three days of the fair, hundreds of people came, and the books sold like hot cakes.

The book fair was repeated from time to time and when cholera struck a few years later, our nurses knew of the town hall, and chose it as their temporary headquarters.

The women's hospital, during the fifty or so years of its existence, should no doubt have been at the top of the uplift list. And with it should go ten or more schools, in the end very largely paid for by government grants. I am afraid we just thought of them as part of our way of life.

The hospital was well-known, not only for the quality and friendliness of its treatment, but also for the fact that it gave equal treatment to the rich and poor, to high and low. But there were amusing pitfalls. If we had told villagers of the hospital, they thought they would get better treatment if they took a note from the Head. They must be encouraged. But the Head had to tread warily, using carefully chosen words: "These villagers are from Kapsi: we told them of the hospital, and assured them you would welcome them and do your best for them."

And building: everyone seems to have taken a turn as architect, but always guided by the experience of Ruben Master, and by the knowledge of the Christian builders. Bishop Wood had put up the first necessary buildings. Dr Mackenzie was good at shoring up some of them when the cotton soil sagged. Dr Mackenzie, I suspect, planned the church at Durgapur, and then fifteen years later added a lovely sanctuary arch. Bricks had to be made on site, where the lime had already been collected and burnt. During the '39-'45 war, we had to get government permits to buy cement. Perhaps I did not rely on letters arriving safely: I sent off applications to Nagpur, to Bombay, and I think even to Madras. Certainly we got two allocations, if not three, and they lasted us to the end of the war. Only after the war was over did I receive a gentle rebuke from high up in Nagpur.

SHIKAR

Sometimes on tour, one went for a week without any meat. At such a time, even a ring dove fallen to the catapult of Robert or Manohar, our bearers, would prove most welcome.

Shikar was one of the occupational hazards of a missionary life, at any rate from the time of Bishop Wood in Chanda to the end of our time in 1953. It was a public service: if a beast was killed, it was skinned, cut up, cooked and eaten in a few hours. Obviously it was shared with the other Christian bungalows, with the servants and their families. If a beast was shot on tour, there were fewer Christians but more villagers to share in the feast.

Shikar was a public duty, but it could only be done in private time, and not when one could be preaching the gospel. In open country, it could be done in the heat of the middle of the day, in the jungle at crack of dawn or before dusk, and before the time for the magic lantern. It was known that we only shot stags. "Shing wallah, sahib, shing wallah!" "It's got horns, Sahib!" Usually it had, but not always: a hind tasted just as good.

In the Mission I had inherited a most useful but horrible little Remington rifle. I well remember my first shot, I think at the Christmas camp at Junona. It was a cheetle, a spotted deer, difficult to see in the undergrowth and quite a way off. I had two young men with me, and I thought I had better do something. Bang! And the beast fell. When we got to it, we found that it was shot through the eye. My reputation was made, and lasted for twenty years, or perhaps even to this day. In the excitement, I had not time to tell anyone I had aimed at the shoulder.

Another day a villager was with me in very deep jungle. We spotted a nilgai – a great pony of a beast – and I had got a shot. Nothing much happened. We tried to follow it, but lost it. (That might, just possibly, have been by intention.) Next day, Bajerao the catechist found the villagers skinning a nilgai.

"One of the villagers has just shot it."

"So …"

Bajerao stood over them as they cut up the beast. Suddenly he pounced, and held up a bullet. The poor villagers had not even got a rifle: it was the Sahib's bullet. Honour was satisfied. The meat was shared. We got our pound of flesh, a haunch of venison.

In our part of the world we were fortunate, in that peafowl were not regarded as holy. They made good eating, and a sporting shot on the ground. The jungle was cleared a few yards back from the side of the road. If you were motoring along and came on peafowl feeding, you only had a few seconds before they were into thick undergrowth. They were best shot in the head with snipe shot.

Shikar

That I think, was my wife's introduction to shikar. We were going down to Ahiri in the little Austin 7 Tourer (sold to us for a song by the widow of Canon Philip: she and her husband were great names in Chanda and Nagpur.) I was in front with the driver, my wife and the dog in the back. I suppose we were going at about 20 m.p.h. when we saw some peacock at the side of the road. I swung round and fired over the head or shoulder or face of my new wife. I got the bird, perhaps in more ways than one. Another evening, my wife was watching me stalk some peacock. Suddenly she looked up, and there was an elephant with its rolling gait coming towards her. It was startling, since we did not know of any elephants in the neighbourhood. It proved to be one of those who had managed to flee from Burma, and had come to help in our jungle.

We had no dog to get duck out of the water, but it was quite simple when one was not much encumbered with clothes. Only once did I nearly get entangled in weed. After the war, Banchory gave me a lovely old sporting rifle. After firing, if there was no wind, one had to step to the side out of the smoke to see what had happened. Anand Master, one of the catechists, was a great shikari. He made the bullets, and filled the cartridges with black powder. I was careful to keep on the right side of him, in case he made the bullets too big!

Ordinarily we did not mix shikar with evangelism. The villagers would have welcomed it but distant trouble makers might have suggested it was force majeur, or it might have been bribery if we had got something. Only once did we take a gun when going preaching. We were staying in the jungle in a huge thatched forest bungalow and had been warned that there was a troublesome bear about. Of course, we saw nothing. But when we got back, we found that the bear had visited my wife and children in the bungalow, but had been routed by our dog and Abdul the cook.

In the evening in a big village we might get 400 or more for the Magic Lantern (as it was to us), the mukka cinema, dumb cinema (as it was to them). We became adept at getting rigged up the twelve feet by twelve feet screen, on bamboo poles supplied in every village. The soil was so hard and dry, that they just dug narrow holes with a crowbar. Often there was no table in the village, so we had to build a Heath Robinson stand for the lantern. After the show, gospels usually sold like hot cakes. During the war, we had to put the price up, when we found them being used as wrapping for sweets at the bazaar. But we may have been wrong: that might have been a way to get the gospels into the most inaccessible homes. Did not Christianity go that way into Japan?

Cuthbert Hall was once called on to kill a cobra in a house – in a room about twelve feet by twelve feet. It looked like being a question of who was quickest on the draw. Cuthbert won, and shot it a few inches below the head. The result: the head went chasing round the room, and that was more difficult to swat than a whole cobra. That feat I could never equal. Our Mission bungalow had a stone-floored open passage. (It was there that Dr Mackenzie once heard a thud, and went and examined Canon J R McKenzie's baby, fallen on the stone floor, without splitting on the ayah. No harm done. His diagnosis must have been sound; did not that baby become a distinguished lecturer at Edinburgh University?) On that passage one night, someone found a cobra. Wanting to be economical and wanting to try out a little Gond axe I had got, I had a go. The axe did little harm, but the cobra was not amused. So I got my gun, stood well away from the bungalow (and the cobra), and fired. We were all terrified: the cobra was nowhere to be seen. We thought of it playing hide and seek in and out of every open doorway. Later, most of it was found about twenty yards away near our kitchen.

Once a catechist and I were in the village at Axapur with the magic lantern. The children were outside in bed. My wife was sitting in the bungalow knitting, on one of those horrible chairs that seem to be made of twisted wires. She heard a rustling and saw a snake coming along the floor. She stood on the rather wobbly chair and called. Abdul came, and did the needful. Later that evening, we were saying our prayers on the not so hot cement floor. Suddenly my wife pointed and there was number two snake coming in. This time I went into action. It does not always do to keep your eyes shut when praying.

In case anyone is thinking of serving in some capacity in India, I should add that snakes are very rare. By now, they may even be "protected", like most of the other wildlife I have mentioned.

On one memorable occasion we were en route to Nagpur, for the Diocesan Council and a happy visit. There were more than a dozen of us in the Mission van all decked out in our best – ironed trousers, lovely saris, I in the whitest of white with a little starch thrown in. (The red dust of Chanda in time got into the skirts of one's everyday cassocks.) Somewhere along the Mul road, we spotted a big boar on the edge of the jungle. The van stopped. Two buses of opposing companies raced passed in a great cloud of dust. As it settled, it was seen that the pig had crossed the road and was standing on our side.

Some time previously, I had carelessly made a little dent in the right barrel. I had hoped the next shot would smooth it out: instead it blew a hole. The local blacksmith, under the direction of Anand Master, had made the repair. I had a huge single shot cartridge for the shot gun – said to be good for tiger close by. In the hurry, it went in. Up went the gun and down went the pig. That was most considerate: if it had loped off into the jungle, where would our finery have been? The pig took up most of the floor space of the van. It seems that even a clean fresh jungle pig has rather a smell. The women in particular protested. We were forced to get rid of the pig in Mul – the only bit of shikar we ever sold.

The Forest Officers, Indian or British, were very kind. They let us shoot anywhere in their domain half the size of Scotland, unless some small area had been let out to someone wanting to bag a tiger.

TIGERS

I think the first tiger we saw was in the dark, with the family in the little open Austin Seven, coming back from Mohourlie. We saw two lights ahead of us and I supposed they were men going out to protect their crops. Then suddenly, the lights were the reflecting eyes of a tiger. With my eyes on the tiger, we ran into a big stone, no doubt left by someone in the middle of the road after cooking their dinner. With the noise, the poor tiger took fright and jumped across the road right in front of us in the little Austin. It seemed as big as the car.

That was not the end of our excitement: near home we had to cross the railway line and the gate was shut. Naturally we slowed down but the brakes had gone; gently we met the gate with a loud clang. That brought out a voluble gatekeeper; he was not complaining, but was apologising that we had found the gate shut!

The next tiger was seen from the bigger van. Some hostel girls were coming back from somewhere and suddenly there was a whisper from David, our driver; "Waagh!" All talk ceased. The van came to a stop. Out onto the road walked a magnificent tiger. For a moment it paused, then - with a "woof" - it was lost in the jungle.

A sad failure must be recorded. It was the only chance I had for a tiger. It happened on the Mul road (see map). There were three or four hostel girls in the Mission van, a catechist who also happened to be a keen shikari, and of course David our driver. I forget what we were going for.

Suddenly we saw a tiger, standing about twenty-five yards away in open jungle. I had the Banchory rifle in the car as well as a shot gun, so I picked up the rifle. I did not want to frighten the tiger by leaning out of the van, so I rested the barrel on the side, and fired. Nothing happened. The tiger looked at us, and walked away.

I knew I would have to send the girls off, and pictured myself with the catechist, playing story-book peek-a-boo with a wounded tiger behind every clump of bamboos. But the catechist went to look where the tiger had been – looking he said, for any hairs or for a hurried paw mark. "Saheb, apen tyalla marila nahi" – "You never hit it." That seemed impossible, but true. Later we concluded that resting the unprotected barrel on the side of the van had varied the vibration.

So I lost my one and only tiger. Yet I can assure readers that when I first shot at Bisley up to 1100 yards for Scotland, I did not miss.

GOODBYE!

We were leaving for good in a few hours time. It suddenly struck me that I ought to provide for a final feast. David the driver and I set off on the Mul road. Before long we spotted a sambur about twenty-five yards off in bamboo. It proved to be a hind, but no matter for our last chance. Within twenty minutes the big beast was hauled into the Mission van, and we were on our way with a feast for all – for the servant families, and for the rest of the missionaries too. It was the first hind I had ever shot. Within a few hours the meat was sizzling on a dozen fires, and Wendy and I, Frances and Jane, had set off for Bombay.

It was goodbye to India after fifteen years, goodbye to Chandrapur and to all our friends. And goodbye means "God be with you."

Charles Copland

Nagpur Cathedral

In 1992 Canon Copland preached in Marathi at the 21st anniversary thanksgiving for the reunion of the Churches. About 1000 in the open air at the Cathedral, under a shamiana.

ENVOI

Perhaps I may end by quoting from the Annual Report for 1952: "We will ever count it a high privilege to have been allowed to labour in this portion of the vineyard." It was said then and it is still true that we rejoice in the great love and staunch friendship that we have found among the people of Chanda. In private I always pray the Lord's Prayer in Marathi, and in giving myself the Holy Communion, I use the Marathi words. Night and day I wear a little silver cross given me in Chanda by David our driver. May the Lord greatly bless and prosper the Church in India.

FROM A FORMER BISHOP OF NAGPUR 1970

Chandrapur has produced good local leadership with prayer and hard work and love of Scottish Episcopal Church missionaries. At present there are 14 ordained ministers who hail from Chandrapur.

It is a matter of pride and thanksgiving that Bishop Arthur Luther, now retired, was elected to the bishopric of Nasik Diocese and later on appointed as Bishop of Bombay and Kolhapur Dioceses in the Church of North India, comes from Chandrapur. Rev. Francis Ramlal is the product of Chandrapur and is serving as a senior presbyter in the Diocese of Bombay. Rev. Wamanrao Ramteke, Rev. B.S. Jadhav and Rev. S.P. Sukare have served the Diocese and now are retired, also come from Chandrapur. Rev. A. Michael, Rev. M.T. Dhotekar, Rev. P.Y. Paranjape, Rev. Premkumar Dhotekar, Rev. Y.P. Bhadake, Rev. Luke Singum, Rev. V.B. Waidande, Rev. Paul Dupare, are currently serving as active ordained ministers in the Diocese of Nagpur, and all come from Chandrapur. The present Bishop of Nagpur, Bishop Vinod Peter, also comes from Chandrapur. The partnership of the Scottish Episcopal Church in God's Mission in Chandrapur continues even though presence of missionary is not possible.

I am told that Durgapur stands in the whole of Maharashtra (a Marathi-speaking State in India) as having highest literacy rate of 96%.

GLOSSARY

Ayah	Child's Nurse
BCMS	Bible Church Mission Society
Bearer	house servant
Bhajan	(Christian) song to universally popular tune
Biblewoman	Indian woman missionary helper
Catechist	Male Indian evangelist
Chandikar	contractor
Chapattis	big thin pancakes
Chaukidar	night watchman
Cheetal	spotted deer
CMS	Church Missionary Society
Crockford	Anglican Clerical Directory
CWMA	Church Woman's Missionary Association (Scotland)
Dak Bungalow	public government lodging
DDT	disinfectant powder – now forbidden
Deroga	police
Dhiver	fisherman, river man
DSP	District Superintendant of Police
DUM	Dublin University Mission
Flunkey	liveried servant
Frangipani	deliciously sweet-smelling tree flower
Girn	complain (Scots)
ICS	Indian Civil Service
Jewar or jewari	food grain, growing three times as tall as wheat
Kabir Panthis	a Punjabi sect of 16th century
Mahars	rather upper class 'untouchables'
Mandli	group of people
MU	World Wide Mothers' Union

Nalla	riverbed, often dry
Nawab	local landowner
NCC	National Christian Council
OMB	Overseas Mission Board (in Edinburgh)
OTC	Officers' Training Corps
Patel	official village headman
Pathan	fierce North-West Frontier tribesman
POW	Prisoner of War
Puggaree	turban
Punkawallah	a man who pulls the room fan
Purdha	segregation of woman
PWD	Public Works Department
Ranee	means queen – local landowner
RAMC	Royal Army Medical Corps
RSM	Regimental Sergeant Major
Sadu	'holy man', probably wandering
Sambhar	big as a red deer
Shamiana	a thin cloth spread over seating for a great crowd
Shikar	shooting, hunting
SPCK	Society for the Propagation of Christian Knowledge (Anglican)
SPG	Society for the Prpagation of the Gospel (Anglican), also USPG – United...
SSJE	Society of St John the Evangelist: Anglican monks
SSMV	Society of St Mary the Virgin: Anglican nuns
Surai	an evaporating cooling water pot
Tank	village pond, often quite big, for irrigation, washing and drinking
Tekedar	small trader
Thurible	a swinging container for burning incense
Turbuz	a huge sort of melon: can pass on river infections
VAD	Voluntary Aid Detachment: semi-trained nurses
Wifie	old woman
Zemindar	rather larger landowner
Zemindari	his holding

INDEX